Keys to CONTENTED LIFE

From
Science, Monks & My Mother

Dr Mary Flaherty

© **Copyright – Mary Flaherty, PhD (2023)**

All original illustrations remain property of the author.

All rights reserved. No part of this publication may be reproduced, stored or introduced into a retrieval system or transmitted by any means (electronic, mechanical photocopying, recording or otherwise) without the prior, written permission of the author.

ISBN 9798387142086

DISCLAIMER:

While this book is based on published science, the information presented is general. The information is presented for reference purposes only and is not intended to diagnose or treat any condition.

The author accepts no liability for any harm caused by the mis-use or misinterpretation of the information presented in this book.

*To my mom,
for her wisdom, kindness and acceptance*

CONTENTS

Introduction	7
1. Importance of a Positive Perspective	13
My Perception of the World is the Lens through which I Live	25
2. Take Note of the Small Things	29
3. Be Present, Meditate	37
4. Acknowledge Sadness and Difficulty	43
Your Flexible Friend - Brains Are Plastic	49
5. Make Good Habits, Break Bad Ones	55
We are Not Rational Logical Beings	67
6. Cultivate Gratitude	73
Our Perception is Not the Same as Reality	79
7. Live Each Day Like A Groundhog Day	87
8. Cultivate Social Connections	97
Losses Loom Larger than Gains ...Mine, Mine, Mine!	103
9. Kindness and Compassion	111
The Brain Seeks Patterns Where None Exist	121
10. Don't Believe Your Thoughts	125
No Matter how we try, our mind will always find problems	151
11. If You Want to Thrive While Alive ...Sleep	153
The Fabricated Past and The Imaginary Future	161
12. Live your Own Story	169
Afterword	191
12 Keys to a Contented Life on One Page	192
The Brainy Bits on One Page	193
Notes	195
About the Author	211

INTRODUCTION

"You have power over your mind – not outside events. Realize this, and you will find strength."

- Marcus Aurelius

I once asked an international audience made up of Sri Lankans, Irish, Americans, Australians, etc. what they wanted most for their children. I got replies such as "a good husband/wife, a good job with a good salary, a good education", etc. I then asked what were these all for…more money? social acceptance? stability? They all finally came to the conclusion that what they wanted for their children, and indeed for themselves boiled down to one thing: to be "content", to be "happy", to "live a good life".

So, what is a good life? What is contentment? What is happiness? How do we make the best of our lot?

From the early philosophers and wise sages, to the stoics and religious traditions and, more recently, the positive psychology movement, people have been pondering the answer to the question "how can we be happier and more content?" We may at some stage ask ourselves the same question when we are thinking of changing career or country or partner. It is easy to feel that we are the only ones who suffer uncertainty and low-level anxiety on a fairly daily basis, and imagine others' lives to be somehow perfect. But we are all faced with the difficulties of making the best of being human.

The great Greek philosopher Socrates boiled it down to one simple command: '*Know yourself.*' Stoicism, popular with the Romans (and enjoying a resurgence in the 21st century) holds that the key to a good, happy life is the cultivation of an excellent mental state, which should be rational and virtuous. Contemporary thinker Alain de Botton, creator of The School of Life, advises that we come to know ourselves, that we treat ourselves as our best friend, being supportive and compassionate to ourselves.

Whatever we might call it - the good life, a life of self-awareness, contentment, peace, happiness, - human beings have been contemplating the 'big' questions of what a "good" life consists of, how to live in the most ideal way and to cope with the strains and vicissitudes of human existence for as long as we know, and probably long before that.

Despite our wishes or efforts to the contrary, most human lives are subject to trials and tribulations such as suffering, adversity, loss, and loneliness, as well as having the potential for ease, enjoyment, fellowship and contentment.

In this book we are going to examine how to make the best of the "bad lot" which is the human condition.

"We have to live in the world as it is, not the world as we wish it to be"

-Kieran Setiya, Philosopher,
Life is Hard, How Philosophy Can Help Us Find Our Way

We all know lots of happy folks, and some unhappy ones too. The happy ones are not happy ALL the time, and even the most habitually miserable of us has experienced happiness at some time in our lives.

Happiness feels good. It is not so much that we can be happy people all the time, but to feel happy a lot of the time would be nice. In much the way that when we work on a garden, we have to make efforts both to keep out the weeds and keep planting the flowers, so too it takes effort to keep ourselves happy and content.

Adopting a positive and accepting attitude to life is good for both our mental and physical health (see chapter 1). We now know that those who take a positive outlook are more likely to have some tried and tested methods and strategies to help them do so. It takes continuous effort, but we are able to influence a large proportion of our own happiness. In his well named book "Learned Optimism" Martin Seligman assures us that we can indeed learn to be happier.

While learning how to be positive is more challenging for some more than others, anyone can pick up the skills required to get there. Whether you're looking to simply to lift your mood, get motivated to exercise or to improve your optimism and relationships, the well-researched ways of being happier, being more positive and content and coping better with the ups and downs of life which are outlined in the coming chapters will help retrain your brain and possibly change your life.

While I will use the terms happiness, positivity and contentment almost interchangeably in this book, I would like to note the differences between them for clarity. Happiness is a feeling, an emotional state often accompanied by positive thoughts and joy. It fades and returns, and is often short-term. Contentment refers to a state of being, and is long-lasting and is essentially a way of life. Unlike happiness, contentment involves a calmness, a peacefulness and is very stable. Nurturing a contented life involves accepting the way things are, and is the foundation for long term happiness.

"Restless, irritated, and discontent, I found nothing okay the way it was and desired just about everything to be different—until I meditated hard on what conditions would make me happy, and found contentment right in front of me."

- Professor Richard E. Cytowic, Neurologist George Washington University

My motivation in writing this book is to consolidate and share some of the most useful and often simple gems which I picked up from 40 years as a psychologist to help anyone cultivate contentment and make the best of life. Scientific findings inform the strategies in this book.

The modern science of psychology is considered to have been founded in the late 19th century by Wilhelm Wundt (1832-1920) and his followers, who conducted the first real experiments in the new discipline. As with every other human endeavour, psychology has had its ups and downs, and has made some phenomenal and practical leaps in the understanding of the human mind and behaviour, as well as taking a few missteps.

As most of the conclusions of Western psychology are based on experimental work done by and on white, middle-aged, educated men, it inevitably produces some limited and biased answers. Having lived in diverse cultures, and having worked in various capacities as a psychologist, from being an academic and research psychologist, to mentoring life coaches and counsellors, I picked up lots of useful (and sometimes not so useful!) information and insights into how we humans navigate our lives.

Real science is slow to make definitive statements about anything. The human mind, being as it is, the most complex and mysterious phenomenon we have yet to discover, has been slow to reveal its workings. Recently, a great many of the discoveries made by psychologists over the last 150 years or so have been called into serious doubt by newer data and more up-to-date experiments.

Some of the bedrocks on which the science of psychology was founded when I was an undergraduate have been shaken, or shown to be downright wrong. Doubtless, some of the insights I share with you in this book will ultimately prove to be partially or wholly inaccurate. However, I have tried to include the best current understanding of the functions of the mind and the practical application of that understanding where I have found it to be useful myself, or have seen its benefits in others.

Of course, long, long before the 'modern', frock-coated gentlemen of Wundt's laboratory conducted their first experiments, countless others had devoted their lives to the understanding of the human condition, the mind and behaviour. The ancient Greek and Roman philosophers, as well as Chinese and Indian sages, came to many of the same conclusions about how to live a good and contented life, centuries, if not millennia ago. Some of these teachings gathered dust for ages on library shelves (the same fate that befalls much of modern psychological research, it must be said!), but other traditions have continued to provide wisdom and solace to their adherents down through the years. Of these, many Buddhist teachings seem as fresh and relevant today as they did 25 centuries ago when they were first embraced by princes and paupers alike as universal medicine for the trials of life common to all human beings.

21st Century psychology, including its most cutting-edge branches of neuroscience and consciousness studies, is highly indebted to, and increasingly informed by, this ancient wisdom. Monks and nuns of many traditions have assisted scientists in their pursuit of understanding of the mind, consciousness and happiness. However, the Buddhists tend to emphasise the practical over the theoretical in order to actually reap the fruits of their teachings. I personally owe a great deal to this way of understanding my own and others' inner worlds, having first discovered the Eastern wisdom of Buddhism and Hinduism as a teenager, and then pursuing them throughout my life, as a daily meditator and yoga practitioner. I have included insights from monks, meditation and yoga teachers which have been of great benefit to me for many decades, and which I have had the privilege of sharing with others, both face-to-face and now through writing.

But wisdom is not the exclusive domain of academics and gurus.

Meet my mom. She was the product of a world without internet, without television, and of a region where electricity was a relatively new and scarce invention - something that lit up the houses of the privileged few, certainly not the cottage into which she was born in South-West Ireland. Her community was self-reliant and resilient by necessity. A trip to a counsellor, or even a hospital was out of the question for most. For most of my mother's family, formal education was limited to a few years of primary school. In that milieu, folk-wisdom - the distilled knowledge of generation upon generation - was the main doctor and guide. Pithy aphorisms and sage sayings gave meaning and context for every occasion and eventuality, from birth, through life's trials and triumphs and even to death. It seemed to me that she had a wise saying or insight for most of the important moments in life; sayings which helped not only to understand the workings not just of the world and of others, but also of oneself.

I'll draw on everything I've got – recent findings from neuroscience and psychology, philosophy, literature, interactions with monks and mystics, my mother's wisdom, personal experiences - to share what I feel are some of the most useful findings to help all of us be happier and more content and to make the most of life.

"Be content with what you have; rejoice in the way things are. When you realize there is nothing lacking, the whole world belongs to you."

-Lao Tzu.

Who Would Benefit from Reading This Book?
Anyone who wants to incorporate strategies into their daily lives in order to make themselves happier and more content and to be more able to deal with the stresses that life inevitably brings. Those with a sense of curiosity about how their mind works and why they sometimes do things that surprise even themselves.

What I Hope Readers Will Get from This Book
I hope you will come to see how much of our behaviour and thinking patterns are due to the way our brains work, and how our brains can change with our actions and thoughts.

More broadly, I want to offer you suggestions of how to gain a deeper understanding of how much you can do on a daily basis to get to know yourself better, to keep a check on your mental landscape, to keep yourself buoyant and more content- and to understand why this is of benefit to yourself and those around you. I hope the book will help enable you to ride the waves of life when the storms hit.

How to Read This Book
You can read any chapter independently. There is a selection of 12 proven and practical ways to help one lead a more contented life. Each of them is tried and tested scientifically. Specific strategies which can be integrated into one's life are suggested. These strategies appear in grey boxes, and are entitled "Give It A Try". While the strategies have been shown to work, they have to be engaged in on a continuous basis. Like exercise, their benefits are only evident when they are done consistently and continuously. However, as with exercise, the benefits are cumulative, and the skills, once learned, become easier to apply. There is no one path to a good life, a contented life, so pick what suits you.

Disregarding the fierce debate as to whether the mind is a product of our physiology – a function of our brains – or something more holistic and mystical – we cannot ignore the fact that the brain is central to both how we perceive the world and how we think, feel and act. For this reason, interspersed between the main chapters (and outlined with a border), I have shared a little about how our brains work, how we interpret the world, how our memory works (or doesn't!) and how our physiology produces predictable glitches in thought and behaviour. As we get better at understanding ourselves and others, we may also get better at managing our lives.

Those interested in reading more detailed accounts of the research mentioned in the text can refer to the notes at the back of the book.

I sincerely hope each of you gets something from this book and that it might help you find more moments of happiness and calm and acceptance in your daily life.

1.
IMPORTANCE OF A POSITIVE PERSPECTIVE

"The trick is in what one emphasizes. We either make ourselves miserable, or we make ourselves happy. The amount of work is the same."

- Carlos Castaneda,
The Teachings of Don Juan: A Yaqui Way of Knowledge

Once when I was a child, I was thrown from a makeshift swing made from a clothesline and fell on my head leaving a severe bump. When I fell on my head, I was aware of the pain and was just about to start crying when my mother who had witnessed the event from the kitchen window immediately came to me and reassured me by telling me that I was some special kind of leprechaun to fall in such a manner. Moreover, the bump on the head I had received was evidence of this. My fear subsided and was replaced with pride of my new found special status as a leprechaun. And I had the evidence to back it up – the bump on my head. My mother was, unbeknownst to herself, acting like a positive psychologist by reframing the situation.

The term "positive psychology" was first coined by Maslow, in his 1954 book "Motivation and Personality." Maslow did not like how psychology concerned itself mostly with disorder and dysfunction, arguing that it did not have an accurate understanding of human potential. Since then, Martin Seligman, Ed Deiner, Barbara Fredrickson and other psychologists have developed it as a new domain of psychology. It is a reaction against past practices, which have tended to focus on mental illness and emphasized maladaptive behaviour and negative thinking. Positive psychology is focused on making the lives of people as fulfilling and positive as possible; it encourages people to discover and nurture their character strengths, rather than trying to correct their shortcomings.

"The chief engine of happiness is positive emotions, since happiness is, above all else, a feeling"

-Professor Sonja Lyubomirsky, University of California
The How of Happiness: A New Approach to Getting the Life You Want

Happiness – How to Get it?
"Mind wandering makes us miserable"

- Professor Dan Gilbert, Harvard University

The core teaching of most ancient Eastern spiritual and philosophical traditions is that fully inhabiting the present is our only pathway to happiness and freedom. It is one of the most elemental truths of existence, and one of those most difficult to put into practice as we live our daily human lives. We are habitually inclined toward the next moment, where anxiety dwells, where hope and fear obscure the direct light of the present reality. We are constantly "nexting" as Dan Gilbert calls it. We tend to sabotage our happiness by looking to find it in the future instead of staying mindful of the present.

The problem is that our civilization and education systems, our parental models and the "escalator system" of work and clambering for promotion - all promise happiness *later*. The future assumes a high degree of reality — so high that the present loses its value.

In truth, our future is made up of purely abstract and imaginary images, none of which can actually be seen, heard, smelled or felt. It is a constantly retreating apparition and we are rushing toward it, only to find that it runs away from us even faster. The root of our ongoing human anxiety is our tendency to live for the future, which in reality is only an abstraction.

Going About Happiness the Wrong Way
The thing is, most companies, parenting styles and schools of management hold with a dogma which insists that work leads to success, and that success will then lead to happiness. This recipe is, scientifically speaking, broken and backwards.

Every time our poor brains get a success, the goal posts move a little further away; get a good grade, but you need a better one next time; graduate from this school, but struggle to get into a good grad school; great job, but need to get that promotion; you reached the client target, but raise the target for next month; get the big house, then get a bigger one; earn more money, lose more weight…ahhgghh! the list is endless.

If happiness is on the opposite side of success, the brain never gets there. We have pushed our achievement of happiness and contentment somewhere far over the horizon into an imaginary future. But the brain actually works the other way around: Happiness and contentment lead to success. In fact - I would say, and so would most people who are quizzed deeply enough - they *are* success.

Why is Positivity Important?
Positivity is a life vest that keeps us afloat and helps to ride the inevitable waves and storms of life. Research confirms that positivity is good for you and others.

In relationships, positive people are more helpful, more sociable and likeable. They have better coping strategies and are more confident.

Positive people are in better physical shape, sleep better, are healthier and heal faster. They have stronger immune systems, lower levels of stress-related hormones and higher levels of growth-related hormones.

Positivity has a beneficial impact in terms of brain chemicals. We see an increase in dopamine (linked to improved learning), and an increase in opioids, which among other things, diminishes our inflammatory response to stress.

Being positive can even help prevent us catching a cold. In an experimental study, Cohen and his colleagues at Carnegie Mellon University examined the relationships between positive emotions and the vulnerability to catching the common cold. With 334 healthy adult volunteers in the community, they first measured both positive emotional experiences, (such as happy, pleased, lively, and relaxed), and negative emotional experiences, (such as depressed, anxious, and hostile), over a few weeks using self-reports. Afterwards, participants were invited to the study lab and exposed to rhinoviruses through nasal drops and monitored in quarantine for the development of the common cold. The researchers found that higher positivity was related to lower risk of developing a cold and fewer reports of symptoms, while negativity was associated with reports of more symptoms. In short, this study showed that experiencing positive emotions was linked to greater resistance to developing the common cold.

Positivity and an optimistic outlook change our brains. MRI scans suggest that a positive mind-set is linked to a better connection of the amygdala to the frontal lobe (which is primary for emotional regulation). While when we are occupied with negative thoughts there is a reduction in this function.

Positive brains tend to be linked to success. While 25% of job success is predicted by IQ, the silent 75% of job success is related to how positive and likeable the person is. Positivity even improves performance. Productivity was found to be 37% higher when workers were happy than when they were induced to have a negative or neutral mood.

In the workplace, positivity enhances creativity and problem-solving and helps reduce burnout. It can even lead to a higher income.

Positivity helps us to live longer life. David Snowdon from the University of Minnesota assessed 678 journals of nuns who had entered Notre Dame in their 20s and kept these journals over the course of their convent life, some 60 years on average. Those who wrote a more positive version of their experience in their autobiographies (in other words biased what Steve Jobs called their "reality distortion field" towards the positive) outlived their more miserable fellows by 7 to 10 years, all else being equal in terms of health markers. Analysis also revealed that positivity was closely related to idea density, which is related to conversation and writing. This research found that higher idea density scores correlated with a higher chance of having sufficient mental capacity in late-life, despite neurological evidence that showed the onset of Alzheimer's disease.

You might ask - which is the horse and which is the cart? Could it be that healthy people are simply happier and not the other way around? Do we simply make choices which contribute to a healthier lifestyle because we are feeling more positive? Possibly, but there may be a biological mechanism underlying this too. When we have negative beliefs, this causes us stress - which in turn causes inflammation. Several studies have shown that inducing positivity can change our biological health markers even if we start out being miserable! It appears that positive thinking and trying to reframe our thoughts with a positive mind-set mediate health benefits not only through our making 'better' and healthier choices (because we are feeling good and hopeful and motivated), but also because of actual biological mechanisms.

We are at our best when our subconscious mind creates a positive sense of ourselves and life in general. Positivity transforms us for the better.

What Determines Our Level of Happiness?

"Happiness is not something readymade. It comes from your own actions"

- The Dalai Lama

A few years ago, when I was researching this whole area of positive psychology, my sister came to visit me in Perth. On arrival at Perth airport from a wet and windy Irish winter, I immediately swept her off to City Beach to enjoy the perfect sunset. After a quick dip in the warm water, she asked me "What does a person in Perth have to be unhappy about? How on earth do you do your positive psychology here?"

Another little story.

When I got my first job as a psychology lecturer at a university in Dublin, I was overjoyed. I loved the campus. I loved the smell of the books in the library. I loved the students. I loved the work. I noticed how my colleagues, some more jaded than others were less enthusiastic than me and certainly less than I expected. I had a memorable interaction (in an elevator, as it happened), with a colleague who told me exactly how many more years, months and days he had left before retirement. He was working my dream job - and he couldn't wait to leave!

The moral of these tales is two-fold. Firstly, we often assume that the external world is predictive of our happiness.

Research has found that **our external world**, however wonderful or awful it may be **accounts for only 10% of our happiness.**

Secondly, **no matter how happy we are at first** with something or someone, **that happiness will fade.** Living in paradise, the perfect job, the partner of my dreams…eventually what psychologists call "hedonic adaptation" sets in. My mother put it more simply when she would stop me from having the fifth bowl of ice cream– "too much of one thing is good for nothing".

We quickly return to a relatively stable level of happiness despite major recent positive or negative events or life changes. As we make more money (or anything else desirable), our expectations and desires rise in tandem. A friend used to make the comparison with the economic theory of "diminishing marginal returns". As I eat more of my favourite chocolate, it loses its appeal. It may even become sickening.

Around 90% of our happiness is determined by how our brains process the world. Of our total happiness, about 50% is inherited. If we had miserable depressed grandparents, we may well have inherited this tendency from them.

But that leaves us with a whopping 40% of our happiness levels which is under our control!

It is both logical and achievable for us to work with this 40% in order to increase our happiness and positivity, and reap all those benefits we mentioned above.

In much the same way that having a healthy body requires constant effort, we need to consciously train and retrain our brains to tread the paths of positivity, to see the leprechaun before the tears and trauma. The various activities in this book are tried and tested ways to do that.

What Would Make You Happier?

"The more one has, the more one wants."

- Benjamin Franklin

Consider for a moment. Maybe we yearn for something bigger, or a more drastic life change. Who wouldn't want to win the lottery? What about a total change of circumstances, move to a sunny climate, or meeting the partner of your dreams? There is no shortage of imaginary scenarios in which we will be happier, swept off our feet into a blue horizon of eternal happiness.

The truth, however, is very different. Let's have a look at things that we think will make us happy but in reality don't - as well as the things that really do.

Looking for Happiness in All the Wrong Places

"Many wealthy people are little more than janitors of their possessions"

- F.L.Wright

Would Winning the lottery make me substantially happier than I am right now?

In 1978, a trio of researchers at North Western University and the University of Massachusetts attempted to answer this by asking three very disparate groups about the happiness in their lives: 22 winners of the Illinois State Lottery — whose prizes ranged from $50,000 to $1 million — 22 non winners and 29 victims of catastrophic accidents, who were now paraplegic or quadriplegic. It was less than a year and a half since the lottery win and the accidents.

The lottery winners reported more overall happiness than the accident victims (an average of 4 out of 5, as compared to the victims' 2.96), but as the authors note, "the paraplegics' rating of present happiness is still above the midpoint of the scale and … the accident victims did not appear nearly as unhappy as might have been expected." And on average, the winners' ratings of everyday happiness for mundane pleasures such as talking with a friend, watching TV, or eating breakfast was actually lower than the accident victims' at 3.33 out of 5, while the victims' averaged answers were 3.48. We adapt to current levels of stimulation, and our judgement of them depends on whether they exceed or fall short of what we have become accustomed to. Overall, the lottery winners were no happier than the non-winners.

This is an example of the phenomenon we mentioned earlier with my job at the university and the beautiful beaches in Perth… hedonic adaptation, the tendency of humans to get used to the things that once made them happy.

A new job or house is great for boosting our happiness but it doesn't last. Children? They may be appealing in the abstract but research says that having children doesn't necessarily make one happier. Neither gender is happier than the other. Even removal of our pain won't improve our happiness in the long haul.

Some Things That Do Make Us Happier – Where We Live and How Spiritual We Are

"When I am in New York, I want to be in Europe, and when I am in Europe, I want to be in New York."
- Woody Allen

Having lived in different countries for extended periods, I began to realize that I was consistently happier in some more than others. It wasn't that the people varied one from another, but that I liked myself more in some countries than others. I think it had to do with 3 factors: how sunny the climate was, perception of safety and acceptance and the relative sense of abundance or poverty within the cultures. I began to wonder if that was a real effect, or was it just me?

As far as where we live and our level of happiness are concerned, perception of safety and level of sunlight *have* been shown to be important.

Every year psychologists collect data from large samples of people all over the world to check their happiness levels. The Scandinavian countries come consistently in the top four or five. While countries like Afghanistan, Lesotho, Botswana, Rwanda and Zimbabwe come in at the bottom. Important factors in our level of contentment are personal freedom, life expectancy and perception of corruption.

Another factor related to location on the planet is Seasonal Affective Disorder (SAD), also called "Winter Depression", a type of depression that's related to changes in seasons. SAD is associated with lack of sunshine. It is a well-recognized condition in the darker countries far from the equator, such as Alaska and Ireland. Symptoms start in the autumn and continue into the winter months, sapping energy and making people feel moody. These symptoms often resolve during the spring and summer months.

Tim Dean, Australian philosopher believes different places have different characters, and so pick one that suits your individual needs (if you could be said to be an individual, given cultural conditioning!).

People who have religious or spiritual beliefs are happier than those who don't, no matter what those beliefs are. Religious or spiritual beliefs give people a sense of meaning. It also gives them a social network. It's less about what you believe than the fact that you have a community, a church, a synagogue, a Bible study group. It's the sense that we are looking after one another that matters. People who are believers have a certain way of thinking: the power of prayer or mantra, rituals, perhaps the belief in an afterlife, that there is a higher or universal power, and that things happen for a reason. These help to reframe potential stressful events.

Social connection, being grateful, getting enough sleep, exercising, living in the present all have the power to make us happy. High self-esteem and optimism make us happy. Being able to take a bad event and reframe as a good event also contributes to happiness. The well-researched ways of being happier and more positive outlined in the coming chapters will help retrain your brain to see the leprechaun and possibly change your life. Read on.

What I thought would make me happy:
- Money
- Fame
- Promotion
- Big House

What actually makes me happy:
- Being grateful
- Kindness
- Sleep
- Being in nature

Today's Outlook: Smiles - With A Chance of Grumpiness

This brings us to another conundrum…how awful we are at predicting what will make our future selves happy…this is called affective forecasting.

"Modern people take the ability to imagine the future for granted, but it turns out that this is one of our species' most recently acquired abilities—no more than three million years old. The part of our brain that enables us to think about the future is one of nature's newest inventions, so it isn't surprising that when we try to use this new ability to imagine our futures, we make some rookie errors."

- Dan Gilbert, *Stumbling on Happiness*

We are all highly vulnerable to mis-predicting what will make us happier in the future. More on this later in the book (The Fabricated Past and the Imaginary Future).

Acceptance

"Some people are born with rose-coloured glasses and a neural architecture that predisposes them to enjoy positive emotions and the best in the world. Other people come into the world with grey-coloured glasses instead of the rose-coloured variety—it's a genetic lottery"

- Professor Jamie Gruman, Organizational Psychologist, University of Guelph,
Boost: The Science of Recharging Yourself in an Age of Unrelenting Demands

Some of us are more naturally happy and others are not. Both dispositions are fine but the key to making the most of life is acceptance. Nothing is positive or negative all the time. If you're not naturally prone to positivity or find yourself dealing with increasing anxiety —don't beat yourself up. It's fine. We live in a culture of smiley emojis. This constant need to appear happy can lead to what is known as Toxic Positivity. Maybe sometimes the emojis that best represent us are more like angry faces or crying faces. They are all fine and all are part of the range of the human emotional landscape.

A Buddhist monk in Perth used to give out "Miserable Awards" to folks who just wanted to be miserable. Acknowledgement and acceptance are the secret. Knowing that pain is a normal part of life, that suffering is a normal part of life, that being down and depressed is a normal part of life – these can all help us learn to accept these lows as natural and normal.

CULTIVATE OPTIMISM

"Nothing characterizes us as much as our field of attention…tell me where your attention lies and I will tell you who you are."

- José Ortega y Gasset, Spanish Philosopher

What Are You Paying Attention To?

An accountant friend of mine who was experiencing difficulties in his life told me that his therapist frequently told him to "stop thinking like a tax accountant". Accountants are adept at using procedures, flow charts, frameworks, worksheets, rules, and checklists to find and solve problems and make sense of chaos. They sift through shoeboxes of receipts to extract errors from relevant documents and discern meaning. Look for an error and you find it. According to the Institute of Chartered Accountants in England and Wales, nearly a third of accountants suffer from depression and anxiety.

Lawyers are also looking for loopholes continuously. They are 3.6 times more likely to be depressed as people in other jobs. In 2016, 28 percent of licensed, employed lawyers in the USA suffered with depression. Why this should be may be multifaceted, apart from the fact that many tend to be driven perfectionists and have huge study debts, they are always looking for discrepancies.

"We handle all of this in an adversarial setting where mistakes are not only pointed out but are relied upon for competitive advantage. That leaves attorneys on edge, and on the lookout constantly. Living like this takes its toll."

—Mark K. Billion, founder of Billion Law,
Consumer bankruptcy firm in Wilmington, Delaware

It is no wonder that depression, anxiety and substance abuse are so prevalent among lawyers and accountants. Their profession requires them to constantly pay attention to the negative.

The good news, on the other hand, is that by focusing on positive aspects of ourselves, others and life, we can enjoy more energy, less depression, more social integration and better health. This is not just wishful thinking – the science behind this very concept is one of the fastest growing areas of research in psychology today.

In his best-selling book "Learned Optimism", Martin Seligman outlines a number of ways in which we can, as the book title suggests, learn to be more optimistic. One of them was simply to write what went well today and why. Seligman and colleagues tested 411 participants in a Randomized Control Trial (the gold standard of the scientific method) on various positive psychology strategies and found that when participants were asked to write down three things that went well and their causes every night for one week, this made people happier (and less depressed) and this effect lasted up to six months later. Other ways that Seligman suggests are challenging negative self-talk and replacing pessimistic thoughts with more positive ones.

A positive mind-set is associated with better health and a lower chance of disease. A review of 15 studies found a 35% lower chance of getting heart disease and a 14% lower chance of early death in people who were optimists. Being optimistic is associated with biological risk factors such as lower blood sugar and cholesterol. People who are optimistic also have better results following surgery, with fewer complications requiring hospital readmission. Optimists have better coping skills when dealing with stress and setbacks. Cultivating optimism may boost our immunity and reduce chances of infection and cancer. Even after considering differences in healthy behaviours, optimistic people had a 15% longer lifespan and 50% greater chance of living past 85 than people with a negative outlook. All in all, cultivating optimism (and it can be cultivated and trained) is good for both our physical and mental health.

Cultivate Optimism

"Your happiness is determined by how you allocate your attention. Changing behavior and enhancing happiness is as much about withdrawing attention from the negative as it is about attending to the positive."

- Daniel Kahneman, Psychologist and Economist

A friend once asked his son "What would you say if I gave you a glass 50% filled with juice?" This was his attempt to see if the boy was tending towards the optimistic or pessimistic end of the spectrum - the glass half empty/half full scenario. He was surprised when his son's answer was - "Thank you".

I think his son had it all worked out. Life that is. Acceptance and gratitude for the way things are is the real secret of a happy life. Think about it. What if everything was all alright? Your marriage. Your finances. Your job. Your health. What if you were perfectly content with all these things as they are, no matter how they look? Accepting things, without trying to change them, is a relief.

However, at times (and maybe often) our minds tend to see the negatives in others, in our jobs, and in our homes.

> **Give It a Try: Take Note of What Went Well Today and Why?**
> 1:
> 2:
> 3:
>
> Every night for next week, set aside 10 minutes before you go to sleep to write down 3 things that went well today and why they went well. This is a way of training ourselves to be aware of, and on the lookout for, the positives in our lives.

*"One evening an old Cherokee told his grandson
about a battle that goes on inside people.*

*He said, "My son, the battle is between
two "wolves" inside us all.*

*One is Evil.
It is anger, envy, jealousy, sorrow, regret, greed,
arrogance, self-pity, guilt, resentment, inferiority, lies,
false pride, superiority, and ego.*

*The other is Good.
It is joy, peace, love, hope, serenity, humility, kindness, benevolence,
empathy, generosity, truth, compassion and faith."*

*The grandson thought about it for a minute
and then asked his grandfather:
"Which wolf wins?"*

*The old Cherokee simply replied,
"The one you feed."*

- Cherokee Metaphor

MY PERCEPTION OF THE WORLD IS THE LENS THROUGH WHICH I LIVE

"All our knowledge has its origins in our perceptions"

- Leonardo da Vinci

We are accustomed to assume that the way we see the world is objective, shared by others and essentially reflects reality. Likewise, we believe that our decisions and subsequent actions are the product of our conscious mind. We'll have a look at some of the ways in which these assumptions are incorrect, and how this might affect our lives.

To help navigate and make sense of our world, we use preconceptions or mental shortcuts—to quickly help us make sense of what we are seeing and experiencing. These mental shortcuts are called cognitive biases by psychologists.

A cognitive bias is a systematic pattern of deviation from the norm or from rational judgment. Individuals create their own "subjective reality" from their perception of the input. An individual's construction of reality, not the objective input, may dictate their behaviour in the world. We humans fall foul of several cognitive biases. I will mention just two.

Confirmation Bias is the tendency to search for, interpret, favour, and recall information in a way that confirms or supports our prior beliefs or values. If I oppose, or support, vaccination, then I will not only seek information to support my point of view. I will interpret news stories in a way that upholds my existing ideas.

Let us take a moment to consider the following statements. Mark them true or false.
1. Most people with exceptionally high IQs are well adjusted in other areas of their lives
2. In romantic relationships, opposites usually attract
3. In general, we only use about 10% of our brain
4. A person who is innocent of a crime has nothing to fear from a lie detector test
5. Usually people who commit suicide have signalled to others their intention to do so
6. On some types of mental tasks, people perform better when they are 70 years old than when they are 20 years old

1, 5 and 6 are true. How did you do?
The thing is most of us have heard statements, read them and digested them so many times that eventually they become the truth for us. We seldom check their validity.

Have a look at these sayings and see whether you agree with them or not.
- Look before you leap
- Birds of a feather flock together
- Absence makes the heart grow fonder

Well, you may just say isn't psychology just common sense after all? ...everyone knows.... But then...
- He who hesitates is lost
- Opposites attract
- Out of sight, out of mind

We generally believe whatever suits our preconceptions, perceptions and conditioning. It is just too hard to deal with cognitive dissonance, discomfort or uncertainty and ambiguity. We accept evidence that supports and is consistent with our beliefs and we ignore information that disproves or is inconsistent with them. We see this confirmation bias in others and hopefully begin to experience it in ourselves as well. From climate change to vaccinations, from trial results to gender, race and political affiliation, confirmation bias affects us all.

Another cognitive bias that we fall victim to is what psychologists call the **Fundamental Attribution Error**. This is the tendency to attribute another's actions to their character or personality, while attributing our own behaviour to external situational factors outside of our control. With others we tend to under-emphasize situational explanations for their behaviour. Basically, others do bad things because they are bad people. But when it comes to myself, I do bad things because of circumstances.

Some guy cuts me off while I am driving. I see his behaviour as being due to his being a jerk. Next day I cut someone off, but I am in a hurry, nothing to do with me being a jerk, just my circumstances. We cut ourselves a break, while holding others totally accountable for their actions. It seems that while we have at least some idea of our character, motivations, and situational factors, we rarely know everything that's going on with someone else. And we often jump to conclusions that are incorrect.

Cognitive biases like the fundamental attribution error and confirmation bias shape how we interpret the world.

How to Avoid Cognitive Biases

Cognitive biases happen due to the natural way our brains work, so eliminating them is impossible. They significantly impact our lives, both positively and negatively. On the positive side, they can help us stay confident in our beliefs and give us a sense of certainty and security. On the negative side, they can lead to poor relationships and poor decisions, and stop us from seeing people and situations objectively.

How to Avoid the Confirmation Bias: Think of examples from your life when you may be victim to this bias. Such as how you seek out or interpret news stories. Are you more likely to believe a story if it confirms your pre-existing views, even if the evidence presented is inconclusive? Or maybe, if you are set on getting a job with a particular company, you may not consider other opportunities that may be better suited to you.

There are a few different ways that we can try to overcome confirmation bias:

- Be aware of your personal biases and how they might be influencing your decision-making.
- Consider all the evidence available, rather than just the evidence confirming your views.
- Seek out different perspectives, especially from those who hold opposing views. For example, read news stories from other sources.

- Be willing to change your mind in light of new evidence, even if it means updating or even changing your current beliefs.

How to Avoid the Fundamental Attribution Error: Think of the last time you thought that someone did something to upset you. For example, a co-worker made a mistake at work. How did you react? Did you think – well, that is the way he or she is? He or she should be fired because they are incompetent?

How often have you really tried to understand the situational factors that could be affecting this person's work?

One tool that can be helpful in combating the fundamental attribution error is gratitude. When you become resentful at someone for a bad "quality" they demonstrate, make a list of five positive qualities the person also exhibits. This helps to see the person through a broader lens.

Another useful tool is listening to what others have to say and why. Become more self-aware. Be more objective and practice empathy.

2.
TAKE NOTE OF THE SMALL THINGS

EVERYBODY SHOULD BE QUIET IN NATURE + LISTEN

NURTURE AWARENESS

Meet Jane. She is constantly busy. She has a high-powered job. She is stressed. She is often away in another world in her head. And she often forgets her husband and children's birthdays. When she is working late or has to travel for work, she feels guilty that she is not with her children. But when she is with her children, she is thinking about work. She gets angry at herself for not being as organized as she imagines herself to be or would like to be. She gets angry at her staff and colleagues for not being as informed and hard working as herself. When she is doing one job, she is already thinking of what she has to do next. The list is long and endless.

Are You Paying Attention?
"My experience is what I agree to attend to"

- William James, Father of Psychology

What we pay attention to shapes our entire experience of the world. This is the foundation of all traditions of mindfulness, which train and cultivate our attention in order to strengthen our quality of presence. The objects of our attention end up, in a subtle but profound way, shaping who we are and framing how we see the world.

We navigate our world by selective attention. We pay attention to what is important to us and tend to exclude from our attention things that don't matter to us. We can easily tune in to a conversation at a party next to us if we hear our own name. We can chat on our cell phone while driving.

But how many times have we met new people at parties or meetings, only to forget their name within seconds. How many times do we inhale our food, only to forget even what kind of sandwich we just ate? Or indeed arrived at work while we planned our day mentally, not remembering a thing about how we drove there. Sometimes it's almost like we are at the movies but asleep. What we are missing are scenes from the movie of our life.

Attention is a limited resource, being able to tune out unimportant details and focus on what matters is an advantage. Paying attention requires focus, selecting specific information while ignoring unwanted information, but most of all, it requires effort.

Our brains cannot be aware of every single thing that happens in the world around us. Big shifts can happen and we may not even notice these changes. Even if it is something as dramatic as when someone changes into another person before our eyes!

In an interesting experiment done in Cornell University, an experimenter posing as a tourist asked a person on campus for directions. When the person started giving directions, two people (collaborating with the experimenter and posing as construction workers), passed by carrying a door. While the "construction workers" passed between the experimenter and the person, the researchers quickly switched the original "tourist" to someone else of the same gender. Only about half of the participants noticed the swap in the person to whom they were giving directions. The experiment was repeated, this time changing the gender of the person asking directions, and even then, many people did not notice that the tourist had changed!

While we might think that we see or are aware of all the changes that happen in our immediate environment, there is simply too much information for our brains to fully process. In many cases, the changes in the visual field are so dramatic that they seem impossible to miss. Yet when attention is directed elsewhere, we are capable of missing both minor and major changes that take place right in front of us.

In another experiment, study participants were asked to watch a video in which two teams, one in black shirts and one in white shirts, are passing a ball. Participants were told to count how many times the players in white shirts pass the ball.

Try it for yourself, before we go on. Jump onto YouTube and search Selective Attention Test. It has had almost 28 million views!

https://www.youtube.com/watch?v=vJG698U2Mvo

Okay, how many times did they pass the ball?

But ... did you see the gorilla? Mid-way through the video, a gorilla walks through the game, stands in the middle, pounds his chest, then exits. More than half the time, participants miss the gorilla entirely. More than that, even after the participants are told about the gorilla, they're certain they couldn't have missed it.

Our brains trick us into thinking we see and know much more than we actually do. We often misremember important events but remain absolutely certain we're right.

The ability to pay attention and detect change around us plays a major role in keeping us safe in our daily life, such as when a car cuts into our lane of traffic. The simple fact is that we have limited attention so we have to pick and choose what we focus on. Expectation and past experience play a role in our attention. As indeed does age, and the use of psychoactive drugs. Distractions also steal our attention - and there are many distractions nowadays.

This attention blindness can cause problems in real world situations, such as air traffic control, driving, and eyewitness testimony. But more importantly in the current context, we often miss small joys that surround us on a daily basis and focus instead on the worries of the future.

SAVOUR LIFE'S JOYS

As the great philosopher Ferris Bueller once said, *"Life moves pretty fast. If you don't stop and look around once in a while, you could miss it."*

Studies which asked people who suffered from depression to spend a few minutes every day doing everything slower and with more attention (showering, eating, walking to work) found their levels of depression reduced as opposed to a similar group who actively did things faster.

> **Give It a Try: Look with New Eyes at Everything**
>
> Next time you eat, hold the food in your mouth a little longer than usual, close your eyes and savour it. Imagine where it was grown, how long it took to grow, the work involved not only in the harvest, but in the delivery to the shop where you bought it, those who displayed it and sold it to you. All the effort and many people that brought your food to you. Try to take a moment before the next mouthful. Maybe even put the fork down to pause.
>
> When driving to work, look at the spring flowers, enjoy the traffic lights and take the opportunity to consciously breathe and take note of how you are feeling.
>
> Notice the sun, rain or shower water on your body ...enjoy the sensations.
>
> Before you go to sleep, take 10 breaths and focus on how your lungs move and note the magic that it continues as you sleep...effortlessly.
>
> Take off your shoes and feel the texture of the sand/floor/water on your toes.
>
> Take 2 pleasurable experiences every day this week and make them as long and intense as possible.
>
> Note the good things in your life that you are taking for granted.

Can You Pay Attention? The Monkey Mind

We spend 30 to 40% of our day daydreaming. How many times have you been out for a run, or chatting with someone, when suddenly you think "did I leave the stove on?", "I wonder who just sent me an email?" The human mind - or specifically our prefrontal cortex, which excels at planning, strategy and problem solving - loves stimulation and in its absence tends to wander, ruminate and worry. It is often why it is referred to as the "monkey mind", swinging from one topic to another, never resting. When left with an abyss, the "monkey mind" turns to the fridge, Instagram or email.

At this very moment, your attention is focused on the words you are reading (hopefully). While you are looking at this sentence, are you giving any attention to the colour of the wall of the room you are in? Are you aware of the position that your feet are in? Until you were asked that question, it's highly unlikely that you were paying attention to either of these things.

In an experiment using the iPhone Web App, Harvard researchers asked 250,000 folks what they were doing and what they were thinking at the random moment they were contacted. 47% of the time they were thinking of something other than what they were actually doing. Indeed, it is likely that you will wander away for a large percentage of the time while you read this.

Unlike other animals, humans spend a lot of time thinking about what isn't going on around them: contemplating events that happened in the past, might happen in the future, or may never happen at all. Indeed, mind-wandering appears to be the human brain's default mode of operation.

Time-lag analyses conducted by researchers suggest that mind-wandering is generally the cause, not the consequence, of unhappiness. Many philosophical and religious traditions teach that happiness is to be found by living in the moment, and practitioners are trained to "be here now". These traditions suggest that a wandering mind is an unhappy mind. And science now supports these traditions.

Give It a Try: What Not to Pay Attention To - Negativity Landmines Worth Weeding Out

Assess your media diet. Cut out sources of information that are causing you distress or low mood.

Reduce social banter/gossip.

Break the rumination cycle – instead go for a swim, jog, do yoga, whatever.

Stop feeding your brain with complaints.

Do not pay attention to negative and unhelpful automatic thoughts.

Cut off or minimise toxic relationships – those that drain you and bring no joy.

Reduce your dealings with negative people.

THE POWER OF RITUAL - ATTENTION, INTENTION AND REPETITION

When I lived in Japan, my home stay family would prepare for a tea ceremony once a month. There was a special house for the ceremony. It was set in a specially designed garden of stone and bonsai and water. The bowls were handmade. As were the little dainty sweets that accompanied the tea. We all wore special kimono. It took hours to prepare and execute. The ritual of preparing and enjoying a cup of tea was elevated to a moment of sublime joy. Far from the styrofoam cup of coffee from Starbucks, taken on the run.

""Time" is the most commonly used noun in American English. We find it, lose it, save it, waste it and spend it. It flies, crawls and stands still. Sometimes we are out of it and other times we claim to have all there is in the world. But just thinking about how much time we waste is enough to rend your soul. Errands and responsibilities build up until the ticks weigh more than the dog."

- Eric Barker, *Barking Up the Wrong Tree*

We can't control Newtonian time, but we can use it to create moments that are meaningful to us internally. Rituals create this magic.

We can use rituals to build meaningful moments that not only help shape our memory of our lives, but also help us to stop and appreciate the moment. They don't have to be religious or spiritual to be both useful and sacred. They simply require intention, attention and repetition. Note that habits are quite different, in that they make things less conscious, less intentional and more automatic. Rituals are mini celebrations. The banal (from a run, or a yoga practice to a meal) can become sacred - with intention, attention and repetition. Athletes are known for having some amazing rituals before they play to boost their confidence…and the rituals work.

"The most memorable periods of our lives are when we break the script."

- Chip and Dan Fredrickson, *The Power of Moments*

I used to teach English as a foreign language. I once planned a class around the question of when the students had their best moments in their lives. All came up with stories of memories that happened in their late teens and twenties. Research shows that when older people look back on their lives, a disproportionate number of their outstanding memories happen in a narrow window: between ages 15 and 30. Why? Because after 30, life can get pretty boring and the months and years tend to blur into one another. After 30, most folks don't do anything as novel as falling in love for the first time, leaving home, travelling on their own, or going to college.

By injecting novelty and intention into our lives, we interrupt the blur. We can not only stretch our internal experience of time, but create more moments worth remembering. And we can do this at a micro level on a daily basis, and on a macro level on a monthly and yearly basis.

Balinese people have their daily rituals to give thanks to the gods; Christians and Jews have their Sabbath; Japanese have, among many other rituals, their tea ceremony. Rituals are there because they are important. Saying grace before dinner. Breaking the Ramadan fast. Rituals around meals go back forever and have profound meaning across almost all cultures and religions.

"Think about rituals that you engage in prior to consumption experiences. What they do, they make us a little bit more mindful about the consumption experience that we are about to have. Because of that, we end up savoring the food or whatever we are drinking more, we enjoy the experience more, and in fact, we're also more willing to pay higher prices for whatever it is that we just consumed."
- Professor Francesca Gino, Harvard Business School

Research backs up the value of ritual. Rituals help couples to report happier marriages. Rituals performed after experiencing losses – from loved ones to lotteries – do alleviate grief, and rituals performed before high-pressure tasks – like singing in public – do in fact reduce anxiety and increase people's confidence. Furthermore, rituals appear to benefit even people who claim not to believe that rituals work.

**Give It a Try:
Make Time More Special and Meaningful with a Ritual**

Be creative in designing your rituals. Any gesture can become a ritual -- just add intention, attention, and repetition. Little rituals help us enjoy and appreciate the moments that make up our life.

Try a day ritual, like a "technology Sabbath", a break from the social media storm.

Give yourself a Sabbath. Take time away from all the duties and ties of life, a day of no errands, no goals, no checklists.

Take a second before a meal with friends and acknowledge how special the moment is.

Celebrate moments of pride, and milestones, such as competing in a sports event, or a graduation with a party.

Break the usual script with a safari on your 80th!

3.
BE PRESENT – MEDITATE

"So long as the mind believes in the possibility of escape from what it is at this moment, there can be no freedom."

- Alan Watts, *The Wisdom of Insecurity: A Message for an Age of Anxiety*

When we feel that vague, constant longing for something beyond the horizon of where we actually are - that apprehension or low-level anxiety - our immediate impulse is to get out of there, to escape. This is invariably a resistance to the present moment as it is. Because we find it difficult to will ourselves to have a different psychological state, like instant happiness, we reach for an easy escape: a drink, a drug, a compulsive scroll through a Facebook feed. We have many escape routes from the present moment. And they are all motivated by the fear that those intolerable feelings will overwhelm us. But by staying within the bounds of the present moment, with all of its discomfort, those feelings dissipate.

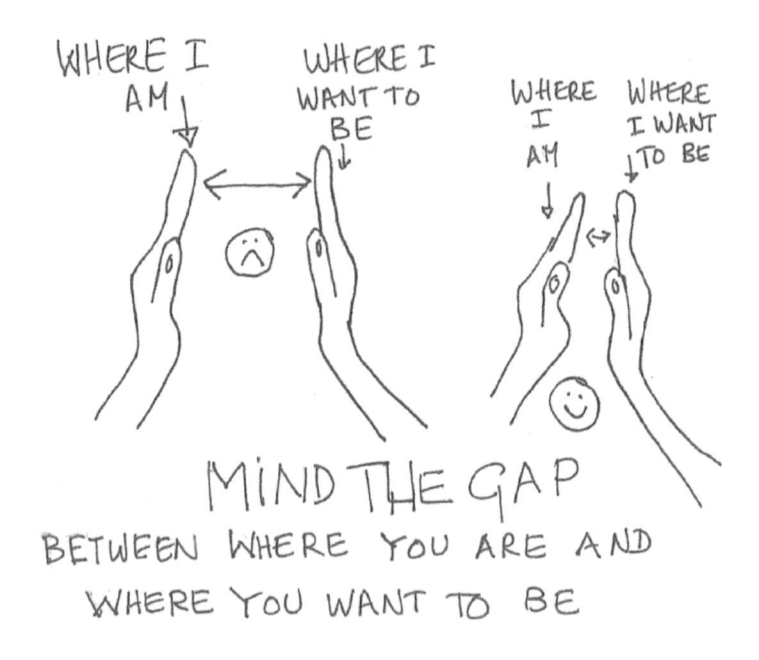

[Illustration: Two pairs of hands. First pair labeled "WHERE I AM" and "WHERE I WANT TO BE" held far apart with a sad face between them. Second pair labeled "WHERE I AM" and "WHERE I WANT TO BE" held close together with a smiley face below. Caption: "MIND THE GAP BETWEEN WHERE YOU ARE AND WHERE YOU WANT TO BE"]

Measuring Misery: The Distance Between Where You Are and Where You Want to Be

A friend once put up his hands and separated them to represent the cause of unhappiness. One hand represented where someone finds themselves right now and the other hand the place where someone wanted to be. And the wider the distance, no matter what the emotions being felt at that moment, the more unhappy one is. We are blessed with brains which are expert at travelling to the past and future, but are doomed to be uneasy in the present moment unless we work at it. However, we have no choice but to live in the present, awash with uncertainty and discomfort as it may be.

Living in the present is one of those most difficult things to put into practice as we live our daily human lives. We are so habitually inclined toward the next moment, where anxiety dwells, we sacrifice the present for an imagined future.

"I fall straight into contradiction when I make "being pleased" my future goal. The more my actions are directed towards future pleasures, the more I am incapable of enjoying any pleasures at all. For all pleasures are present, and nothing save complete awareness of the present can even begin to guarantee future happiness."

- Alan Watts, *The Wisdom of Insecurity: A Message for An Age of Anxiety*

What keeps us from happiness, many religious and spiritual traditions and now many experimental studies argue, is our inability to fully inhabit the present. Scientists have shown how we tend to sabotage our happiness by looking to find it in the future instead of keeping mindfulness of the present. The problem is that our society, education, our parental models all adopt an "escalator system" where more education, more work, more money and more clambering for promotion all promise happiness *later*.

The future assumes a high degree of reality and importance — so much so that the present loses its value. However, the future is made up of purely abstract and imaginary images, none of which can actually be seen, heard, smelled or felt. It is a construct of our minds, very rarely turns out to be the way we expect and usually has a completely different impact on us than we imagine from our current viewpoint. Human anxiety has its roots in living for a future which is no more than an abstraction.

We are in a constant state of postponement. We spend all week waiting for the weekend. We believe that the weekend will make us happier. And it does. For a while. But it's not so much because it's the weekend, but because we stopped waiting. Same with a holiday. How many times have we counted down the days to a holiday, only to find that at the end of the holiday we are looking forward to going home!

Meditation or mindfulness can help to bring our full awareness to our present experience and is not only one of the best ways to improve our attention, by helping us to be in the present, but has also been shown to make us happier and healthier. Let's take a short look at its many flavours and the evidence for its physical and psychological benefits.

Meditation - From Monks to Modern Psychology

"Don't just do something, sit there"

- Thich Nhat Hanh, Buddhist monk

When I was a graduate student at a university in Japan in the 80s, one of my psychology supervisors was researching the effects of meditation on the brain waves of Zen monks who had meditated for 1, 10 or 30 years plus. These were the days before Jon Kabat-Zinn and the whole mindfulness craze and meditation was largely unknown in the West outside of academic and religious circles. Research on the area was in its infancy. Curiosity led me to one of the two main temples of the Soto sect of Zen Buddhism, Eiheiji in northern Japan, where my supervisor arranged a week of meditation with the monks for me.

Days started at 3.30am and involved a continuous stream of 40 min *zazen*, or sitting meditation sessions. The simple instruction was to just allow my thoughts to come and go, and not to grasp on to any of them. We were encouraged to live in the moment.

I tried to be aware of my thoughts and empty my mind. But they kept coming. "How long has it been since we sat? Twenty minutes? Did I just hear the sound of the gong to finish the session? What will they give us to eat today?" And on and on.

The series of gongs and drums were the sweetest sounds to my ears, bringing each sitting session to an end. Of course, there was nothing special about the sound of the gong. It was simply that it signalled an end to my waiting.

While all the intent of silencing the streaming monologue that filled my mind seemed to fail, I remember how the residue of my zazen sessions resonated with me for weeks, maybe months afterwards in that I had developed the habit of watching what was going on in my mind when I was not actually focusing my attention on something. I became an intermittent observer of my consciousness. Worrying about money, recounting past events with anger or fear, making up stories of what might happen next … all my thoughts seemed to be pretty negative.

I began to be a silent observer of my endless thoughts. I wondered how would it be if I could turn down the volume, or better again turn it off. Would I still be me looking at "me"?

These journeys into my consciousness intrigued me.

After many 10-day silent Vipassana meditation retreats and decades of practice in a more compassionate approach to meditation within the Thai Forest tradition, I realized that:
- a lot of what goes on in my mind is a repeat of yesterday's (and the day before, and the day before that) script
- my thoughts lead to my feelings. Good thoughts lead to happy feelings and bad ones to anger and fear
- I am most content when I am present in this moment
- I became calmer and less reactive
- my mind wanders and that's fine
- I could do this almost anywhere and more-or-less anytime

It is an interesting development that an ancient meditation practice from a monastic system aimed at the lofty goal of spiritual liberation is now presented as an innovative method of therapy, helping us to cope with the stresses of modern life and even be more productive in the workplace. Whatever the motivation, the evidence that it works is strong.

While there is a wide range of styles of meditation and mindfulness-based therapies in modern psychology (such as Mindfulness-Based Stress Reduction (Kabat-Zinn), self-compassion (Kristin Neff) and loving kindness (Fredrickson)), I will consider the evidence on meditation in a generic fashion.

Benefits of Meditation/Mindfulness

A student I once supervised in Australia gave a mindfulness App to all her friends who were also mothers and partners of FIFO workers (Fly In Fly Out…which means the partners work on the mines and come home every 3 weeks or so for a week's holiday). It is well recorded and researched that the life of a FIFO parent at home can be challenging. The mother cares for the children for 3 weeks and is hoping for some relief when the partner returns. Meanwhile the partner has been working hard for 3 weeks and is hoping for some relief when he gets home. Poor formula for a balanced relationship. My student found that the mothers who used the mindfulness App on a daily basis coped much better in terms of communication and dealing with anger issues than those who did not.

There is now a plethora of research on meditation and mindfulness showing it to make real changes in the brain. It encourages parasympathetic nervous system activity, thus reducing stress as well as improving focus, cognitive flexibility, memory and concentration. Meditation helps train the mind to focus on the present, making one less likely to ruminate on anxious thoughts that can fuel low mood and depression. It increases positive emotions while reducing negative ones and helps us to regulate those emotions better. It helps improve our self-awareness by increasing our ability to examine and observe our thoughts, feelings and bodily sensations without judgement. It helps treat heart disease, lower blood pressure, reduce chronic pain, improve sleep, and alleviate gastrointestinal difficulties.

Meditation is not stopping thoughts…they will keep coming. We learn to look at the thoughts with a relaxed focused mind, a non-judgemental and kind mind. We begin to see the pattern of the storyline we keep telling ourselves and learn to take it more lightly. We watch for negativity, nervousness, discontent. We watch for thoughts that appear to justify or explain this unhappiness, but in reality, cause it.

Give It a Try: Take Rest - Live in the Present - Meditate

Take a moment to sit back and do nothing. Get very comfortable. Take time to make sure each part of your body is at ease and if you have pain somewhere, watch it and welcome it as you would a guest. This may take time. Mentally scan your body from your legs up to your head, noting if there is pain anywhere and send some care and compassion there. Begin to watch your breath and note whether it is going in or out.

Imagine that you are holding two very heavy shopping bags, the one on the left says PAST and on the right FUTURE. Now imagine yourself dropping the PAST bag onto the floor and the feeling of lightness in your arm and shoulder. Same with the one with FUTURE from your right hand. Feel the weightlessness in your body and the lightness.

Continue to watch your breath. Notice when the mind becomes engaged in some thoughts (and it will). Just watch them and once you notice them return to the silent space of breath and awareness. Allow the mind to settle into the observer role rather than the processor role. It's tough to do, but you can get a glimpse of it.

Start with giving it about 5 minutes and build it up over time.

There are many YouTubes, Apps and websites with free access to meditations. If you can't find anything that suits you, this is one by Perth-Based Buddhist Monk Ajahn Brahm that I really like - https://bswa.org/teaching/friday-night-meditation-6-july-2018/
Have a look around the net to find meditations that suit you.

A friend who teaches meditation told me that people often ask her *How often should I meditate?* She told me that when she recommended beginners to sit for a few minutes three times a week, they would put it off on Monday till Tuesday, on Tuesday till Wednesday and so on. In the end, she found that people found it most effective when she advised them to *mediate every day*, if only for 5 minutes each day.

Give It a Try:
Incorporate Mindfulness and Being Present into your Day

Practice being present briefly and regularly through the day. At traffic lights, notice the things around you, the sounds or your body position and tension, not simply waiting to get into the future and for the lights to turn green.

Note when you are feeling frustrated, or angry and rather than initiating an internal negative monologue "why me?", label the feeling "frustration" or "anger". And watch it. This allows the emotional brain, the amygdala, to cool down. It loses its strength and power. When we name our feelings, we tame our feelings!

Practice meditation and living in the present until they become personality traits.

4.
ACKNOWLEDGE SADNESS AND DIFFICULTY

"Some things just hurt"

- Sharon Salzberg, Author

Forty years before the philosopher Kieran Setiya published his book "Life is Hard", psychiatrist Scott Peck opened his ground breaking and best-selling book "The Road Less Travelled" with the simple line: Life is difficult.

"Life, friends, is hard – and we must say so. It's harder for some than it is for others. Into each life some rain must fall, but while the lucky dry themselves beside the fire, others are drenched by storms and floods, both literal and figurative"

- Professor Kieran Setiya, MIT,
Life is Hard, How Philosophy Can Help Us Find Our Way

We will all at some point in our lives suffer pain, sickness, loss, failure, rejection, disappointment and, if we get that far, the ailments of old age. There is no denying it and it is naïve to pretend otherwise.

There is no way out of it. To be human means we will suffer. Sometimes we need to feel the sadness and pain that life evokes.

Life is full of ups and downs. But we hate feeling down. We even hate when others are feeling down or in pain. I remember difficult incidents in my life, such as a health scare or when I was fired from my job (for being a foreigner and female, but that's a long story and not for now!), and friends advising me that *it'll be alright*, or *it is all for the best*, or *the universe has made it so* or *things happen for a reason*. None of these comments helped. It was when someone sincerely listened and acknowledged the pain and hurt I was going through, that I felt heard and was comforted. It didn't make the bad feeling go away, but rather it gave it permission to be felt.

"The only way out is through."

- Robert Frost's poem *Servant to Servant*

Feeling Bad About Feeling Bad Can Make You Feel Worse!

"All real living hurts as well as fulfils. Happiness comes when we have lived and have a respite for sheer forgetting. Happiness, in the vulgar sense, is just a holiday experience. The life-long happiness lies in being used by life; hurt by life, driven and goaded by life, replenished and overjoyed with life, fighting for life's sake. That is real happiness. In the undergoing, a large part of it is pain."

- D.H. Lawrence

It is not uncommon in our society to ignore sad and painful feelings or to struggle to interpret them in a positive way. But when we have the expectation that we're supposed to feel happy and positive all the time, we imagine that there's something wrong with us when we feel down.

Research suggests that embracing negative emotions can make us feel better, while pressure to be positive can actually make us feel worse. A large study carried out at the University of California tested the link between emotional acceptance and psychological health in more than 1,300 adults in the San Francisco Bay Area and the Denver, Colorado, metropolitan area. They found that people who habitually accept their negative emotions experience fewer negative emotions and better psychological health than those who don't. The results suggest that resisting acknowledgement of our darkest emotions, or judging them harshly as somehow "wrong", can end up making us feel more psychologically stressed. By contrast, when we allow bad feelings, like sadness and disappointment to run their course without judgement, we are left more psychologically healthy.

"How we approach our own negative emotional reactions is really important for our overall well-being. People who accept these emotions without judging or trying to change them are able to cope with their stress more successfully."

- Brett Ford, Assistant Professor of Psychology, University of Toronto

We learn from sadness. When we are living through disquieting winters in our lives, we need to stay with them to explore and feel the emotions. Joan Didion explored the experience of mourning the death of her husband in her marvellous book *The Year of Magical Thinking*. At first she found herself in a miserable numb state a lot of the time. Over the course of a year, there were gradually more glimpses of hope. Our strength in such situations is to acknowledge them, accept with an open hand what we are feeling and not try to fight it and not to replace it immediately with something else.

From her experience of living through a difficult period, Katherine May, wrote the following

"[Since childhood] we are taught to ignore sadness, to stuff it down into our satchels and pretend it isn't there. As adults, we often have to learn to hear the clarity of its call. That is wintering. It is the active acceptance of sadness. It is the practice of allowing ourselves to feel it as a need. It is the courage to stare down the worst parts of our experience and to commit to healing them the best we can. Wintering is a moment of intuition, our true needs felt keenly as a knife."

- *Wintering, The Power of Rest and Retreat in Difficult Times*

Give It a Try: Notice Feelings of Pain

We have bodies and thus all suffer pain at some stage of our lives. Some more than others. Some pain is acute, some chronic. When you are in pain, take time to meditate on the pain. Become an objective observer of your body. Focus on all parts of the body that are in pain and all parts that are not. When negative thoughts come when you meditate - and they will - just let them be. Befriend them. Return to a more spacious awareness of your body and breath.

"None of us are invincible. But in how we garden the winters of the soul, we find the summer of our strengths and the bloom of our fragile aliveness."

- Maria Popova, *The Marginalian*

Give It a Try: Accept and Acknowledge When Life Is Hard

Notice the next time something happens in your life that brings pain, or sadness, or loneliness. Stay with the feeling and see what happens. Try not to judge it or to make it go away. Try to remain open and accepting to the experience, despite the discomfort.

"Don't surrender your loneliness so quickly, let it cut more deep. Let it ferment and season you as few human or even divine ingredients can. Something missing in my heart tonight has made my eyes so soft, my voice so tender, my need of God absolutely clear."

-Hafiz

Give It a Try: Acknowledge the Pain of Another

Sometimes we can't even cope with the pain that a friend is going through and we feel a desperate need to try to somehow "make it right". Notice if you are prone to denying the pain of another.

If a friend is going through a hard time, suffering pain, or loss, rather than immediately trying to make them feel better with encouraging comments like *"it will all be alright"*, (or the one I really take umbrage with *"What doesn't kill you makes you stronger"*) listen and acknowledge their pain.

Give It a Try:
Imagine Ways in Which Life Could Be Even Harder

My grandmother had goitre. My mother had an overactive thyroid. I recently saw a photo of myself and noted that my throat looked larger than normal. I immediately checked in the mirror and nothing seemed to have changed. It must have been the lighting in the photo. Suddenly I felt elated that I didn't seem to have goitre.

Imagine some of the things that could have gone wrong today and how you are so lucky that they didn't. This is a kind of "pay it forward" gratitude exercise. We will all suffer in the long run. No getting away from it. But today maybe things that could have gone awry didn't. I didn't crash the car. I didn't get stung by a jellyfish. I didn't cut myself preparing the dinner.

"In the depths of winter, I finally learned that within me there lay an invincible summer"

- Albert Camus

YOUR FLEXIBLE FRIEND– BRAINS ARE PLASTIC

"Any man could, if he were so inclined, be the sculptor of his own brain."

- Santiago Ramon y Cajal,
Father of Modern Neuroscience

NEUROPLASTICITY

AFTER YEARS OF TALKING ABOUT TROUBLES, THINKING ABOUT THE DIVORCE, WATCHING THE NEWS....

AFTER YEARS OF THINKING ABOUT THE GOOD TIMES, NEW BEGINNINGS, WATCHING COMEDIES ...

O ur brains are constantly changing as we experience and adapt to the world around us, influenced moment to moment by our experiences, our thoughts and our emotions.

As noted in the introduction, we should remember that our tendency to be happy or not has some basis in our genetics, up to 50% of our happiness or otherwise can be innate. Unavoidable circumstances in our environments are responsible for another 10% of our total happiness or unhappiness. So, what can we do to optimize the remaining 40%?

When we tune in to the evening news, or read the newsfeed daily, we are bombarded with bad news. Today's quick search for the headlines leaves me with "shooting inside mall leaves 14 wounded"; causalities mount up in Ukraine; growing refugee crisis, COVID continues to kill…and on it goes. Feeding my poor brain with only fear and anxiety.

The fact is that the constant exposure to sounds, images and stories of a negative and frightening nature like these cause the brain to be rewired in such a way as to leave it more prone to seeing negative and frightening patterns in the world around us. Eventually this can leave us almost no choice but to conclude that we can't trust anyone and that the world is generally unsafe.

Of course, the converse is also true, exposing ourselves to and re-emphasising positive happenings and experiences makes us more likely to perceive the world at large as safe and friendly.

Psychology and neuroscience have shown that the adage from physical exercise, that we "gain what we train" is as true for our perceptions and mental world as it is for our heart, lungs and muscles.

Our brains are pattern-making organs, made up of 100 billion nerve cells called neurons. These neurons have spidery branches that reach out and connect to other neurons to form a neural net. From the time we are children, our brains are rapidly forming associations, making assumptions and drawing conclusions about everything we experience through our senses, thus creating connections in our neural net. Our brains gather information and steer our thoughts and behaviour based on these associations, assumptions and conclusions.

Our neural networks are constantly changing as we live through and adapt to the world around us, influenced moment to moment by our experiences, our thoughts and our emotions. In other words, what we feed the brain is what the brain will pay attention to. Our brains are plastic, having the ability to respond, adapt and continually change depending on what they are fed.

"Thought changes structure."
- Norman Doidge, Psychiatrist and Psychoanalyst

Norman Doidge, the author of "The Brain That Changes Itself" became interested in the plasticity of the brain and collected a number of personal stories to find out what it means.

"I saw people rewire their brains with their thoughts, to cure previously incurable obsessions and traumas."

What he is saying is that he saw evidence that the brain can change itself, not if we do nothing, but if we are willing to make an effort. When we learn something new, we create new connections between our neurons. We rewire our brains to adapt to new circumstances. This happens on a daily basis, but it's also something that we can encourage and stimulate.

When we read negative news on a regular basis, we are giving our brains a particular kind of input. When my mother chose to reframe the sore bump on my head as a leprechaun's trademark, my brain was fed another story.

Our brains are like a snowy hill in winter. Aspects of that hill—the slope, the rocks, the consistency of the snow—are, like our genes, a given. Now, when we ski down that slope, we will end up at the bottom of the hill by following a path determined both by how we steer our skis and the characteristics of the hill. Where exactly we will end up is hard to predict because there are so many factors in play.

However, what will probably happen the second time we ski down the same slope is that we will, more likely than not, find ourselves somewhere or another that is related to the path we took the first time. And if we spend our entire afternoon skiing down the same paths, we will create tracks in the snow that are very difficult to get out of. And those tracks are no longer purely a product of our genetics, but of our behaviour and experience. In the same way, neural circuits, once established, tend to become self-reinforcing and self-sustaining.

Neuroplasticity refers to the brain's ability to adapt – or to get stuck. It works both ways, it gives rise not only to mental flexibility and growth, but can also lead to mental rigidity and stagnation. The mental "tracks" that get laid down can lead to habits, good or bad. If we make the effort to continuously practice piano or math problems, we will become more adept at these tasks. But if we repeatedly develop poor mental habits, such as paying attention to bad news, we will become prone to perceiving and expecting bad news.

Is it possible, once "tracks" or neural pathways have been laid down, to get out of those paths and onto different ones? Yes - according to a wealth of neuroscientific research, but it is difficult, because once we have created these tracks they become "really speedy" and very efficient at waring down our neural ski track. So, as Dr Norman Doidge reiterates, we need to be aware of what slope we have chosen and choose wisely if we can.

My mother, unbeknownst to herself was a neuroscientist. She knew that reinterpreting my fall in a positive way (before I could begin to experience and rehearse it as the minor tragedy it could have been for an eight-year old), by having me see myself as something magical like a leprechaun, she was helping my brain to break the circuit of a negative reaction so I would interpret my fall not as a disaster, but as something positively awesome. She reframed many such "disasters" during my childhood.

Neuroplasticity – Ski Down a Positive Slope

"Among other things, neuroplasticity means that emotions such as happiness and compassion can be cultivated in much the same way that a person can learn through repetition to play golf and basketball or master a musical instrument, and that such practice changes the activity and physical aspects of specific brain areas."

- Andrew Weil, M.D., *Spontaneous Healing*

Do we ever meet a friend and she shows us photos from the rainy days on her holidays or from her divorce? Not usually! We only see the sunshine shots and the wedding photos. Why not do our brains the same favour and focus on the happier memories?

Take a moment to conjure up some sensual images…take note of how your body feels, the sounds, sights, smells while you ponder the following:

> When things went your way, even better than expected
> When you felt at peace and serene, content
> When you felt really proud of yourself
> When something made you laugh

Note how you felt after this little imaginary journey.

Neuroplasticity – Be More Objective

"Because of the power of neuroplasticity, you can, in fact, reframe your world and rewire your brain so that you are more objective. You have the power to see things as they are so that you can respond thoughtfully, deliberately, and effectively to everything you experience."

- Professor Elizabeth R. Thornton,
The Objective Leader: How to Leverage the Power of Seeing Things as They Are

How many times have you driven to a specific destination, one that is familiar and routine, and arrive minutes or hours later without remembering much about your trip?

When we are overreacting, misjudging people and situations, often it is because we are responding automatically, based on the assumptions, associations and conclusions that have been hardwired in our neural ski slope about particular people or particular situations. Repeated association between an event and an emotion has left its neural mark on us. *"Neurons that fire together, wire together"* as Canadian neuropsychologist Donald Hebb famously said.

We all experience the world from our own viewpoint. Therefore, our immediate response to the world becomes subjective, shaped by our cultural conditioning, our thoughts, our desires, our fears and our past experiences. We alone are responsible for how we respond to everything we experience in our world. Our opportunity to increase our objectivity lies in our ability to own our cognitive appraisal process and reduce our automatic reactions.

"You fill a bucket drop by drop. You clear your mind thought by thought. You heal yourself moment by moment. Today I make one drop, clear one thought, and get present to one moment. And then I do it again."

- Lisa Wimberger, *New Beliefs, New Brain: Free Yourself from Stress and Fear*

Neuroscience reveals that with the brain's neuroplasticity, we all have the capacity to change our responses – to situations, thoughts, bodily sensations, social interactions or any other form of stimulus that we experience. By heightening our awareness, we can become more objective, and, rather than reacting to stimuli, respond to them and thus ski down a different slope. Every time we notice and interrupt our automatic reactions and choose a different response, we are loosening those neural connections and reinforcing new pathways that will allow us to create behaviour and feelings that we want, not those that we end up regretting.

"A sense of 'new' — seen, heard or experienced for the first time — causes the brain to generate enriching levels of the neurotransmitter noradrenaline, which has remarkably beneficial effects on the networks of your brain. Curious people live longer because of these positive brain effects; they do not become jaded by the grey predictability and over-familiarity of the worlds we create for ourselves. The habit of curiosity is a power-tool for the mind that opens vistas, perceptions, thoughts and opportunities that are closed to the uncurious mind".

- Professor Ian Robertson, Co-Director of the Global Brain Health Institute

Take Home Message:
Develop the Habit of Curiosity to Feed Your Brain
Get curious. Say out loud to yourself "I wonder if or why…." "What if…", "Supposing…"

Avoid labelling something as boring, always see it as a door to an exciting new world.

Expand your world by reading different kinds of books and magazines, listening to different kinds of music or podcasts.

Push out of your comfort zone to learn something new and difficult.

Learn a new language, make music, make up a dance, visit new places, take a different way home, etc.

5.
MAKE GOOD HABITS, BREAK BAD ONES

"We are what we repeatedly do.
Excellence then, is not an act, but a habit."

- Aristotle

I recently asked Michael, a wonderful healthy and happy elderly man who I got to know during the COVID pandemic, what was the secret to his upbeat and youthful demeanour. He told me *"Make good habits and lose bad ones"*.

Understanding a little about how our brain deals with habits can help us to follow this wise advice.

Habits are behaviours which are carried out automatically because they have been performed frequently in the past. This repetition creates a mental association between the situation or cue, and action or behaviour, which means that when the cue is encountered the behaviour is performed automatically.

Automaticity has a number of components, one of which is lack of thought. The brain actually changes once a new habit has been established, and thus needs fewer neurons to initiate and carry out the habit. We can't be ambivalent about changing habits. We need to repeat the action again and again so that the neurons that now fire together, wire together in a different way.

Any behaviour that can be reduced to a routine is one less behaviour that we must spend time and energy consciously thinking about and deciding upon. Habits therefore free up time and energy for other matters. Habits emerge because our brains are constantly looking for ways to save effort. An efficient brain allows us to stop thinking constantly about basic behaviours, such as walking and choosing what to eat or wear so we can devote mental energy to being creative and to seek out new stimulation.

When a habit emerges, the brain become more efficient (and needs fewer resources) because automatic patterns take over. Voilà…neuroplasticity!

The habit loop, as Charles Duhigg refers to it in his book "The Power of Habit", requires us to develop triggers (or cues) and rewards. Rewards can be intrinsic or extrinsic. Intrinsic rewards are those that originate from within the person, and extrinsic rewards are those that originate from something beyond the person. An extrinsic reward often has monetary value - such as a salary increase, bonus, award, or public recognition - and is usually tangible or visible. An intrinsic reward is an internal reward, a psychological boost that we achieve from completing a task or project successfully. Intrinsic rewards mean that the task itself *is* the reward, and we are motivated to repeat that task for its own sake. We feel better. And this latter type of reward is better in the long run for helping us to keep a habit going.

So, when I throw my yoga mat in the same spot at the same time every morning, I know it is time to practice. I also know that after the practice I will feel better. I have done this for years. I now don't even have to think. The cues are in place (yoga mat, same time, same place, same part of the room), and the routine (the actual yoga practice) and the reward (generally feeling good) follow automatically. Eventually over time, the reward will be doing the practice itself. I should mention that when I first started this habit, I rewarded myself with chocolate (extrinsic reward) and would only allow myself to eat some after I had done the yoga practice.

Over time, this loop—cue/trigger, routine, reward—becomes more and more automatic. The more often my brain uses the loop, the deeper the behaviour is etched into the ski slope of my brain. It becomes ingrained— to the point where the behaviour itself becomes more and more automatic. As Duhigg explains, *"habits emerge without our permission."* (Beware – this applies to bad habits as well as good ones!)

Research conducted at University College London by Phillippa Lally and colleagues found that it takes 66 days of performing an initially new behaviour to become automatic. So keep at it!

Establish Good Habits, Break Bad Ones

"Every morning when I wake up, I experience an exquisite joy —the joy of being Salvador Dalí— and I ask myself in rapture: What wonderful things is this Salvador Dalí going to accomplish today?"

- Salvador Dalí

Habits aren't destiny. Habits can be ignored, changed or created, or replaced. But the reason the discovery of the habit loop is so important is that it reveals a basic truth: When a habit emerges, the conscious mind stops fully participating in decision making. It stops working so hard, or diverts focus to other tasks.

Give It a Try:
What Habit Would You Like to Make A Part of Your Life?

Years ago, a friend of mine said casually to me that if I wanted to incorporate anything into my life, I needed to do it every day. This really made me think. Did I want to make exercise a part of my life? Did I want to be kinder? Did I want to play a musical instrument? Did I want to be more positive about myself and others?

Think about a habit that you would like to establish as part of your life. Maybe for you, it's reading, gardening, running, being kind, or something else you'd like to do more of.

To get started and create a habit, you need to repeat the behaviour in the same situation. It is important that something about the setting where you perform the behaviour is consistent so that it can cue the behaviour. Choose context cues, for example, when and where. I do my yoga as soon as I get up in the same place every morning.

Identify a cue for this habit - Make the new behaviour as easy as possible.

Identify a routine - Any opportunities to leverage the change? Like working from home …opportunity for lunchtime walk?

Identify a reward – Maybe start with an extrinsic reward, like a smoothie after your walk. Develop rewards. Both short and long term. After a week of walking, maybe you can treat yourself to dinner at your favourite restaurant.

> Create multiple habit loops to account for changing situations, like if it rains, I can do an exercise class from the internet rather than the walk outside.
>
> Can you piggyback your new habit onto a pre-existing routine? Maybe you already go out for lunch every day and you can go for a longer walk to get there.
>
> Keep doing it for at least 66 days until it becomes automatic.

Breaking or Changing Habits Is Very Difficult

"Habits never really disappear. They're encoded into the structures of our brain, and that's a huge advantage for us, because it would be awful if we had to relearn how to drive after every vacation. The problem is that your brain can't tell the difference between bad and good habits, and so if you have a bad one, it's always lurking there, waiting for the right cues and rewards".

- Ann Graybiel, Neuroscientist, MIT

We generally don't intend to create bad habits. For example, families usually don't intend to eat fast food on a regular basis. But they do it once a month, then once a week, then twice a week, until it becomes normal.

"We know that a habit cannot be eradicated—it must, instead, be replaced."

- Charles Duhigg, *The Power of Habit*

I was a coffee addict; I would have three or four cups several days a week. I was getting more and more anxious and found my heart pounding in bed. I was unable to get a good quality sleep. I knew I had to give it up. I had to replace my habit of coffee with something that was not so detrimental to my sleep. I broke the habit down. The cue that triggered my coffee routine included a location - coffee shop, a time of day - during work for a meeting, and after work with my friends. The reward was a nice feeling, a caffeine kick, the presence of certain other people, the nice cup, the coffee shop. Identifying the reward can be difficult, as it is sometimes masked among other things. I realized I really liked the feeling of treating myself.

Studies indicate that once habits are formed in the brain, they become encoded in the structures therein, and can never truly be eradicated – only replaced with a stronger habit.

I had to change my habit. I recognized the cue ("I want to go to a nice coffee shop, and use a nice cup and meet a friend"), I identified the reward ("I feel relaxed and like the ambiance of the coffee shop") but found an alternative routine ("Instead of the coffee, I have mint tea…always in a nice cup"). The caffeine kick was missing in the reward, not a small sacrifice. But eventually, (after many months of relapses) I automatically had mint tea when meeting friends in nice cafes. The new routine became automatic. The real reward was the warm feeling of being with good friends!

For a habit to stay changed, three things are important: people must believe change is possible; that the change is important and that they build support. It is difficult to break any habit even when you are motivated to do so. If you are ambivalent about breaking it then you will be less likely to succeed. Our odds of success with breaking bad habits go up dramatically when we make our intention public and commit to changing as part of a group.

I knew I could not go on with the anxiety and sleeplessness I was having as a result of my caffeine intake. It was important for me to stop. I told all my friends that I no longer drank coffee. They never offered me coffee again in their homes. I had changed my story. The reason Alcoholics Anonymous (AA) is so successful is that it instils in its members the 'belief' that small wins are possible and important. At the same time AA provides the essential support and constant reassurance through their group processes.

> **Give It a Try: What Bad Habit Would You Like to Break?**
>
> When a friend of mine moved to the south of Spain, she began drinking a glass of wine a couple of nights a week with new friends. Then she found herself having a glass each night, something she didn't normally do. Some nights it became two glasses, then most nights. She told me that she wanted to change this new habit but at the end of the day in the sunshine a glass of wine always sounded fantastic. A second glass usually did too.
>
> Think about a habit that you would like to break. Maybe it's something you'd like to do less of - like smoking, refraining from dessert before bed, reducing social media time or watching less TV.
>
> Make a plan for what you'll do when you face the obstacles. When the urge hits and you don't have a plan, it's too late.
>
> If you have a setback, start again. Failures can be just as important as successes when trying to change habits. It's not an easy task, and I'm sure every one of us has tried to quit something and failed, or tried to do something positive and failed. The key, of course, is to not just give up after failure, but to reset your resolve, to analyse what went wrong and why, and to plan to overcome those obstacles the next time. If you do miss once, or twice or three times, don't give up. Just figure out why you missed, and plan to beat that obstacle next time. Be as consistent as possible from then on out, until the new habit is ingrained.
>
> Build meaning into replacing the bad habit. Keep doing it until it becomes automatic. Tell people about it.

Get support - your mom, your sister, your best friend, your boss. Maybe an online friend. Best yet, join a support group or an online forum full of people doing the same thing.

Keep a log. A log helps you succeed because it reminds you to be consistent. It keeps you aware of what you're actually doing. It motivates you, because you want to write good things in that log.

Focus on one habit at a time. Devote all of your energy to that habit change, and once it's on autopilot, move on to the next one. Don't forget to be kind to yourself. Breaking bad habits can be hard. Let yourself off the hook now and again. One cake now and again is okay. One day off from your running routine is fine. My mother used to say *"A little bit of what you fancy does you all the good in the world"*. But remember she said "a little bit"!

CHANGING HABITS TO CHANGE YOUR LIFE

"A slight change in your daily habits can guide your life to a very different destination. Making a choice that is 1 percent better or 1 percent worse seems insignificant in the moment, but over the span of moments that make up a lifetime these choices determine the difference between who you are and who you could be. Success is the product of daily habits—not once-in-a-lifetime transformations. You get what you repeat."

- James Clear, *Atomic Habits*

Some habits matter more than others. "Keystone habits", a term coined by Charles Duhigg, are habits that automatically lead to multiple positive behaviours and positive effects in your life. What the Stoics may have called things that help us live a "good life". What Aristotle saw as leading to excellence. These are habits that when changed, set off a chain reaction that extends to all aspects of our life.

Keystone habits can influence how people work, eat, play, live, spend and communicate. They start a process that, over time, transforms everything. Some examples of keystone habits might be having social gatherings (enjoyable and nurture relationships), exercising regularly (good for our health in the long run), tracking what we eat (over time this too is a habit and healthy eating is a choice), meditating, sleeping, positive thinking. These habits change our brains and in so doing, our lives. In fact, this book is all about knowing our minds and changing them for the better, not just for ourselves, but for those around us too.

Of course, keystone habits can be both positive and negative and they have a compounding influence on our lives. If I decide to do my best at work, over time, my career will benefit and I will enjoy it in and for itself. If I commit to helping and being a bit kinder in each interaction, this can result in a network of strong and broad connections over time.

On the other hand, if I allow myself to get stressed at any frustration, for example being impatient whenever I find myself in a queue, this will become a habitual reaction. The more I think of the negatives in others and in life in general, and the more I complain that things are not the way I want them to be, the more my brain will interpret the world this way.

Our habits can compound for or against us.

All big things come from small beginnings. The seed of every habit is a single, tiny action. But as that action is repeated, a habit sprouts and grows stronger.

"Breakthrough moments are often the result of many previous actions, which build up the potential required to unleash a major change. This pattern shows up everywhere. Cancer spends 80 percent of its life undetectable, then takes over the body in months. Bamboo can barely be seen for the first five years as it builds extensive root systems underground before exploding ninety feet into the air within six weeks.

Similarly, habits often appear to make no difference until you cross a critical threshold and unlock a new level of performance."

- James Clear, *Atomic Habits*

Give It a Try:
Focus on Your Keystone Habits and Refine Them

Spend time considering what keystone habit you would like to change or refine, or indeed implement in your life.

For example, introducing a new routine like exercising; eating a meal as family; being kinder with others. Write it down. Maybe share it with others. Identify the cue, the reward and the routine and then implement it. Repeat and repeat.

My new friend Michael is a living example of someone who cultivated keystone habits in his life.

Forget About Goals, Focus on Keystone Habits Instead
"Don't just aspire to make a living, aspire to make a difference."

- Denzel Washington

For many years, I set goals. I trained enthusiastically for races, doing 5 km runs so I would be ready. After the race, however, my running regime went to the dogs.

Goals are about the results you want to achieve. Keystone habits or systems are ways of approaching life, are about the processes that lead to those results.

A friend who lives by goals, asked me during the pandemic how I get a sense of achievement on a daily basis and what goals I had set for the lockdown. I meditated daily, I walked. None were for a sense of achievement or goals, but are in fact my lifetime keystone habits.

A friend told me she spent years going to Weight Watchers to manage her weight. The focus of the method for weight loss was on reducing the "points" consumed (a proxy for calories), and there was a regular "weigh-in". Both these are highly goal-oriented, extrinsic rewards, and my friend's weight kept fluctuating, despite the group pressure. However, once she stopped focusing on "points" and getting her weight to a certain level and instead shifted her attention to incorporate the lifestyle changes that she was learning from Weight Watchers her weight stabilised. She focussed on things like not eating the entire bread basket when she went to a restaurant; watching portion sizes and knowing when she had had enough. In other words, she became successful at her aim of keeping a healthy weight when she exchanged her goals for keystone habits.

If you're a musician, your goal might be to play a new piece. Your keystone habits might be how often you practice, how you break down and tackle difficult measures, and your method for receiving feedback from your instructor.

Goals are good for setting a direction, but keystone habits are best for being content and healthy and happy in the long run. A handful of problems arise when you spend too much time thinking about your goals and not enough time designing your keystone systems.

Imagine you have a messy room and you set a goal to clean it. If you summon the energy to tidy up, then you will have a clean room—for now. But if you maintain the same sloppy habits that led to a messy room in the first place, soon you'll be looking at a new pile of clutter and hoping for another burst of motivation. You're left chasing the same outcome because you never changed the system behind it. You treated a symptom without addressing the cause.

The main problem with goals is that they can restrict our happiness. The implicit assumption behind any goal is this: "Once I reach my goal, then I'll be happy." The problem with a goals-first mentality is that we are continually putting happiness off until the next milestone. When we are content with the process of life rather than the product, we don't have to wait to be happy. We can be content at any time. True long-term thinking about life is goal-less thinking. It's not about any single accomplishment or set of accomplishments. It is about the cycle of endless refinement and continuous acceptance and adjustment to the way things are.

Give It a Try: Write a Personal Constitution of How You Want to Live and Who You Want to Be

When I first read Stephen Covey's book "Seven Habits of Highly Effective People" I was really taken by his recommendation to develop a "Personal Mission Statement." Never before had I actually taken the time to sit, ponder my values and the things that were truly important to me, and then to write my own constitution, something that would help me when faced with difficult decisions and keep me on a sincere path. Like the constitution of a country, it would help shape my future, my decisions and my aspirations. It really helped to write it down in point format and carry it in my wallet. (I also carry a few quotes that lift my spirit in moments of despair).

Do for yourself what the founders of many countries have done for their countries. To this day, the US Constitution is the one document that the Supreme Court uses to make its decisions on difficult aspects of the law.

A Personal Constitution gives you a pathway that is built on the values that are important to you and that you refuse to compromise on. It moves you in a clear direction which you've chosen for yourself. As your constitution will reflect your deeper ideals, before you draft one, identify values that define you, and that you wish to maintain or develop.

Revise and review it from time to time. Keep reminding yourself to stay true to yourself, especially when the winds of life push you in different directions and you need a compass - or an anchor.

Give It a Try: Letter from The Future

Think about writing a letter to yourself now as if you were 80 years old and tell your younger present self what was meaningful in your life and the things you were proud of.

Be careful to not be influenced or pushed in a direction that isn't right for you because of echoes of what someone said to you like: "You should be doing this", "You'd be an an idiot not to take this opportunity," "Consider what others might think".

And be really careful of the voices in your head, or of other people, which remind you to "be reasonable". Sometimes you may need to break the mould of your existing habits, and be "unreasonable" in order to achieve the change you really need to develop.

Advice from your imaginary older self may help you identify what is really important for you on a life-long timescale, rather than being overwhelmed by matters which seem urgent and important in the short term.

"To be yourself in a world that is constantly trying to make you something else is the greatest accomplishment."

- Ralph Waldo Emerson

WE ARE NOT RATIONAL OR LOGICAL BEINGS

"It is not to be forgotten that what we call rational grounds for our beliefs are often extremely irrational attempts to justify our instincts."

- Thomas Huxley.

We tend to go through life in the belief that we are responsible for our actions and that we are rational, logical beings with clear insights as to why we make given decisions and take given actions.

Psychological science, especially cognitive psychology has, over the last 50 years or so, shown that we humans are far from rational. In fact, we all carry built-in mental glitches and design features which can lead us to behaviours which are quite surprising – even to ourselves!

Our Brains Work like Lawyers, Not Scientists

SCIENTIST — MAKES OBSERVATIONS, GETS FACTS — THEN DRAWS CONCLUSIONS

LAWYER — HAS THE OUTCOME DECIDED — THEN FINDS INFORMATION TO SUPPORT DECISION

When my partner and I decided to buy land to build a house, we had criteria that it had to be south facing, not on a slope, and easy access to a main road. We saw a site in the south west of Ireland, and as we liked it so much, we bought it. It was north facing, on a steep slope and on a by-road. But we justified our buy, citing things such as the forest that surrounded it, the fact it was near the sea, and so on, factors we hadn't even considered before we fell in love with the site.

Why did you choose the job you are doing? Did you choose it because it is appealing or did it become appealing because you chose it? In other words, did you create the evidence after the fact to help you make sense of the choice?

Be it with a partner or a job, or maybe even ordering a meal, we are not the objective; rational creatures we like to think we are. We often make up reasons for our choices AFTER the fact. This kind of motivated reasoning is rampant in our psychological lives and it is also highly adaptive.

There are 2 main ways to the truth about ourselves – We can generate our self-image either rationally and objectively like a scientist, or we can start out with a conclusion about events and then find means to justify that conclusion- rather the way a clever defence lawyer would do to "prove" her client was innocent.

An objective scientist gathers all the evidence they can about a topic and then examines it carefully, weighing up evidence for and against before coming to a conclusion or taking action. Do I choose A or B? I thoroughly and consciously examine all the benefits and costs of both and then weigh them up and come to an objective conclusion.

The lawyer, on the other hand, starts from a pre-decided outcome (she has to prove that her client is innocent, for example) and then sets about finding evidence and arguments to prove it. I have made up my mind, (perhaps unconsciously or subliminally, as to what I want to believe) that I want to live in Bunbury and now I go about finding reasons to justify my pre-decided conclusion. Most of the time all of us are more likely to act like a lawyer rather than a scientist.

Let's look at a decision process from both points of view.

Ming is thinking of getting married. The only problem is that he can't decide between two lovely women. Kate is his ideal match, she is well educated and well-travelled, as he is, comes from a good family and the same culture etc. Josephina is stunningly beautiful, really good fun and loves to dance all night and has no desire to settle down.

If Ming is acting as a scientist, he will most likely get down on one knee and propose to Kate, she is, after all, the most likely to become a stable and long-lasting partner.

However, Ming is really, really attracted to Josephina. When his friends ask him who he wants to marry, he will tell them that Josephina is wonderful, and that he's sure she will settle down and become a devoted wife if he can only show her how much he cares for her.

Ming is free to act either way. He can be his own scientist, or lawyer.

Many of the great philosophers were well aware of our human tendency to rely on feelings rather than reason. Jean-Paul Sartre, French existentialist philosopher gave a wonderful example of this. A young girl finds out she is pregnant and is not sure what to do. She chooses to either go to the priest or her girlfriend for advice on having an abortion. She thinks that their help will give her what she needs to make an objective decision. She has already made her decision herself when she chooses who to ask, but she believes she is being rational in seeking help.

The Scottish philosopher, David Hume "was deeply attentive to the curious way we very often reason from, rather than to our convictions. We find an idea nice or threatening, and on that basis alone declare it true or false. Reason only comes in later to support the original attitude" (The School of Life).

```
┌─────────────┐   ╭──────────────╮   ┌─────────────┐
│ SCIENTIST   │  ( HOW DO I      )  │ LAWYER      │
│ STYLE       │  ( CHOOSE A      )  │ STLYE       │
└─────────────┘  (  PERFECT      )  └─────────────┘
                 (    PARTNER?   )
                  ╰──────────────╯
```

✓ GOOD JOB   SUPER ATTRACTIVE
✓ WANTS KIDS   ↓
✓ SENSE OF HUMOUR   ✓ I BET THEY LIKE KIDS
✓ GOOD LOOKING   ✓ DOESN'T MATTER THAT
        ↓   THEY ARE UNEMPLOYED
    A GOOD   ✓ I KNOW THEY ARE SERIOUS
    CATCH   BUT I LOVE THAT SMILE

"Reason is, and ought only to be the slave of the passions, and can never pretend to any other office than to serve and obey them."

– David Hume, Philosopher

Traditionally, psychologists assumed that our behaviour and our feelings were conscious and consistent. But we now know that at a subliminal level our behaviour and feelings depend on how our body is feeling (hormones, neurotransmitters and other factors over which we have no conscious control), the social and emotional contexts, what happened previously, etc. It seems the psychologists are finally listening to some of the wise philosophers.

Let's have a look at some examples of the ways our brains, unbeknownst to ourselves do strange things! And how we justify things like a lawyer might…after the fact.

Fooling Ourselves –
We Generate Our Beliefs in a Creative Manner

I am a fan of Kerry football team and Kerry is playing Dublin in the All-Ireland football final. I will see every tackle the Kerry players make as athletic, enthusiastic and playing fair, even if it is very boisterous (no matter what they do). I will be more inclined to interpret the exact same style of tackling by the Dublin guys as foul or dirty play. I see what I want to see. This has a fancy name in psychology - confirmation bias - as we mentioned earlier. The lawyer in my brain finds evidence to confirm my pre-existing bias.

If I am a doctor and a drug company is "encouraging" me to prescribe their drug to my patients by giving me a trip to Bali, I am more likely to prescribe their drug than another drug which benefits me less... but I don't do this consciously. I am acting like a lawyer. If asked, I could give any number of reasons as to why this company's product is the best one.

Indeed, political psychologists highlight denial of global warming or discrediting its science as examples of this kind of bias. People will only process the information about climate shifts that conforms to their pre-existing beliefs and feelings. If accepting all the evidence that climate change is real, they may have to make significant and uncomfortable changes to their perception of the world as well as to their lifestyle.

Prejudice against different races is born out of similar mechanisms.

Take Home Message: Think of a bias you may have, against a team, a country, a political party, a race, etc. Consciously be a defence lawyer for them finding evidence to support them. Challenge your cognitive bias.

6. CULTIVATE GRATITUDE

"Gratitude turns what we have into enough."
— Anonymous

I WANT TO EXPRESS MY GRATITUDE FOR.....

PRETEND EVERYDAY THAT YOU ARE GIVING AN OSCARS SPEECH

Let me introduce you to two older people.

Entitled Ed is 80. He has not been very well for about 40 years. Two of his daughters live with him and one of them, Mary is his full-time carer. But Ed constantly complains that his family are not good enough to him, that Mary doesn't really know how to care for him. Ed had a good career, a kind wife who he never noticed, because he was always a little unwell. His other children visit him at least once a week. He would like if they visited more.

Grateful Grace is 84. She lives alone with her cat. She has some health issues, but she is always thankful that she can get up in the morning and make herself a cup of tea. Her children live all over the world. She is delighted when one of them calls her and always tells them that it makes her day. She is grateful for everything – when one of her children comes to visit, to have such lovely neighbours, to have a cat, to have a home. Although her health means she can't move as fast as she used to, she is grateful that she can still clean her house herself. She recalls her life story as one of gratitude.

Entitled Ed and Grateful Grace are presented as a vignette to offer a lens through which to see aspects of ourselves and maybe annoying versions of who we could have been. If you are anything like Ed, read on.

Gratitude for Better Health

When we express gratitude, we acknowledge the goodness in our lives. And in this process, we usually recognize that the source is at least partially outside ourselves and many times due to chance. Incidentally, when things go wrong or not the way we want them to go, it is also partly due to chance.

Martin Seligman and many other giants in positive psychology research have shown consistently that gratitude is strongly associated with greater happiness. Gratitude helps people feel more positive emotions, relish good experiences, improve their health, deal with adversity, and build strong relationships.

Whether we are applying it to our past (retrieving positive memories and being thankful for elements of childhood or past blessings), the present (not taking good fortune for granted as it comes), or the future (maintaining a hopeful and optimistic attitude), we can train our very malleable brain to *"plant the flowers, and the weeds will disappear"*, eventually cultivating a brain that tends towards the grateful rather than the complaining narrative. In narrative therapy, a form of psychotherapy that seeks to help patients identify their values and the skills associated with them, people are encouraged to tell the story of themselves, and that story can highlight whatever is most appropriate and serves them best (see chapter 12).

Gratitude is a way for people to appreciate what they have instead of always reaching for something else in the hopes it will make them happier, or thinking they can't feel satisfied until every physical and material need is met.

Research on Gratitude

Two psychologists, Dr Robert A. Emmons of the University of California, and Dr Michael E. McCullough of the University of Miami, have done much research on gratitude. In one study, they asked 200 participants to write a few sentences each week, focusing on particular topics and divided them into 3 groups.

One group wrote about things they were grateful for that had occurred during the week. A second group wrote about daily irritations or things that had displeased them, and the third wrote about events that had affected them (with no emphasis on them being positive or negative).

After 10 weeks, those who wrote about gratitude were more optimistic and felt better about their lives. Surprisingly, they also exercised more and had fewer visits to physicians than those who focused on sources of aggravation.

Another leading researcher in this field, Dr Martin Seligman, a psychologist at the University of Pennsylvania, tested the impact of various positive psychology interventions on 411 people in a well-designed Randomized Controlled Trial, the gold standard of scientific research. When their week's assignment was to write and personally deliver a letter of gratitude to someone who had never been properly thanked for his or her kindness, participants immediately exhibited a huge increase in happiness scores and decreased depressive symptoms. This impact lasted for a month. (Incidentally, two of the other interventions – writing about three good things that happened each day and noting why they were good, and using signature strengths of character in a new way – made people happier (and less depressed) up to six months later. These strategies are mentioned in chapters 1 and 12.)

Research on the positive outcomes from writing a letter of gratitude has been replicated many times. It does four things:
- Gratitude disconnects us from toxic, negative emotions and the ruminating that often accompanies them. Writing a gratitude letter "shifts our attention" so that our focus is on positive emotions.
- Expressing gratitude helps us even if we don't explicitly share it with someone. We're happier and more satisfied with life simply because we completed the exercise.
- The positive effects of gratitude writing are like compound interest. You might not notice the benefit of a daily or weekly practice straight away, but after several weeks and months, you will.
- A gratitude practice trains the brain to be more in tune with experiencing gratitude — a positive plus a positive, equals more positives!

Seligman also studied the relationship between gratitude and depression. He asked people to take note of positive things that happened to them during the day over a certain period of time in a gratitude diary. Could be big things, like love for their family or something small, like noting it was a sunny day. He also asked them to record how deep their depression was. Results showed that those who had reported the deepest depression initially also reported the greatest beneficial effects.

Other studies have looked at how gratitude can improve relationships. For example, a study of couples found that individuals who took time to express gratitude for their partner not only felt more positive toward the other person but also felt more comfortable expressing concerns about their relationship.

Managers who remember to say "thank you" to people who work for them may find that those employees feel more motivated to work harder. David Cooperrider coined the term "Appreciative Inquiry" which focuses on strengths rather than trying to rectify weaknesses in a company. The idea was that "problem solving" hampered social improvement and would not allow new ideas to emerge. "Appreciative Inquiry" focuses on what works, uses artful creation of positive imagery, and has all members of an organization understand and value the most favourable features of its culture.

Two examples from my own life. One head of department that I worked for years ago was continuously telling us at staff meetings what a great team we were and he would detail what our strengths were. We had more publications, more students and less turnover while he was in charge than all the others under whom I worked at that university. On the other side of the coin, I remember having a boss who continuously told the staff we were not working hard enough, were not recruiting enough students and were not saving enough resources in the university. I explained the underpinnings of Appreciative Inquiry to her and at the next staff meeting, we were welcomed with a mention of some strengths of staff in the department.

Ways to Cultivate Gratitude

Gratitude helps people refocus on what they have instead of what they lack. And, although it may feel contrived at first, this mental state grows stronger with use and practice. We literally retrain our brains to focus on the positive in our lives.

Give It a Try: Thank Someone Mentally

If you have no time to write, just think about someone who has done something nice for you, and mentally thank them. You can even thank folks mentally like those who make your life more comfortable – the bus driver, the person who delivers the avocados, and the ones who grow them, etc.

Give It a Try: Write 3 Things You are Grateful for Right Now

1:
2:
3:

Give It a Try: Write a Thank-You Note

Days after Albert Camus received the Nobel Prize in Literature, he sent his childhood teacher a beautiful letter of gratitude, that was included in the last pages of his book "The First Man".

Dear Monsieur Germain, ...when I heard the news, my first thought, after my mother, was of you. Without you, without the affectionate hand you extended to the small poor child that I was, without your teaching and example, none of all this would have happened. I don't make too much of this sort of honour. But at least it gives me the opportunity to tell you what you have been and still are for me, and to assure you that your efforts, your work, and the generous heart you put into it still live in one of your little schoolboys who, despite the years, has never stopped being your grateful pupil. I embrace you with all my heart. - Albert Camus

You can make yourself happier and nurture your relationship with another person by writing a thank-you letter expressing your enjoyment and appreciation of that person's impact on your life. Be specific as to what you are grateful for and why.

Once in a while, write one to yourself.

Give It a Try: Imagine That Someone or Something In Your Life Currently Is Taken Away And Is Gone

Could be your wife, your husband, your most important friend, your home, your pet, your health. For a moment, imagine they are gone. In detail, close your eyes and take a moment as to how your day, your life would look without them. Nurture gratitude for what they give to you.

Give It a Try: Build Gratitude Rituals into Your Day

Consider ways you can ritualize how to bring gratitude to your meals (a prayer, a quote), your home (flowers, keep tidy, etc.), your health.

Give It a Try: Keep a Gratitude Diary

Keep a gratitude journal and a few times a week, consider both what you have and what life would be like without what you have. Think also of all the bad things that did not happen today which very might well have come to be. Reflect on what went right or what you are grateful for. It can be just as powerful to be thankful for things that *didn't* happen. How lucky I was that I didn't fall off my bike this morning.

Let your legacy be one of appreciation and gratitude like Grateful Grace.

OUR PERCEPTION IS NOT THE SAME AS REALITY

"Reality is only a reflection of our own intentions, biases, knacks and desires."

- Abhijit Naskar, Neuroscientist, *Mission Reality*

When I used to show this cartoon to first year psychology students and ask them what they saw, I got answers ranging from Tweetie bird with a glass, to a chair standing behind a table with a glass on top to a cleaning lady from the back with her bucket. Thing is, we may be looking and experiencing the same visual image, the same lines on a page, but we see different things.

Our perception of the world is not the same as objective reality. And we can never really know the perceptions of others. For example, we may be surprised to learn that some folks who have lost a limb still "feel" the limb that has been amputated. And that not all people can recognize faces. Some people who we may accuse of being unfriendly simply cannot recognize faces. This condition, called prosopagnosia, is more common than you might think. As many as 2.5% of the population have it, as it so happens.

The things we focus on when we interact with our world change us in turn. With our actions, we create changes in parts of the brain in the somatosensory cortex that are dedicated to specific parts of the body. A pianist will have more representation for the hands and fingers in the cortex of their brain than someone who never touched a piano. A blind person will have enhanced sensitivity of the skin.

And so our perceptions shape us both psychologically and physically. Positive thinking can lead to enhanced creativity, staying focused, problem-solving skills, and overall mental productivity. On the other hand, negative emotions can lead to slower response times, memory impairment, and decreased impulse control.

We Can Change the Lens Though Which We View Reality

We use mental shortcuts or cognitive biases to navigate life. We make the interpretation of a situation fit our ready-made conclusions on a regular basis. And these can be and are highly protective and useful.

"It is not reality that shapes us but the lens through which we view the world that shapes our reality."

— Shawn Achor, Author

If we can change the lens through which we view reality, we can change not only our happiness, but our relationships, creativity, confidence, health and many other aspects of our lives.

If we know that our beliefs, our cognitive biases, conditioning, and the story we tell ourselves about who we are (more on this in chapter 12) are so volatile and without firm foundation, then we can make choices as to how we want to think and live. This is very good news and extraordinarily liberating.

Austrian neurologist, psychiatrist, philosopher, author, and Holocaust survivor Viktor Frankl made the memorable assertion that *"everything can be taken from a man but one thing: the last of the human freedoms – to choose one's attitude in any given set of circumstances"*.

The trick to resetting what we are used to perceiving as reality is awareness and consciously paying attention. Have you ever, for example, driven to work (maybe for many years) and not noticed the names of streets or shops that you passed every single day?

Our Reality Can Be What We Choose or What We Are Conditioned to Perceive

Things are not set in stone and our reality is constructed from a set of perceptions. Perception is malleable and therefore subject to change. If we become aware of some of the processes going on in our mind, we may be able to steer our reality in a new, more desirable direction. But this takes deliberate awareness. Mindfulness or meditation are excellent tools in this process.

We know how we feel by reconstructing sensations (from memories), the data at hand (how you are feeling right now) and pre-existing beliefs and expectations. And what we believe is very important.

"Whether you think you can, or you think you can't – you're right,"
- Henry Ford

Attitude and belief determine success or failure. A study on school children clearly demonstrates how this works. Kids were first assessed, then ranked. As part of the study, only the psychologists knew that the students ranked 1st and 2nd, 5th and 6th, 9th and 10th, etc. were put into class A, while students ranked 3rd and 4th, 7th and 8th, etc. were assigned to group B.

The teachers were naïve to this. They expected the students in group "A" to be brighter simply because of the label of their group and treated them accordingly. Similarly, they expected the "B" students to be lazy and less bright and so also taught them as per their expectations. At the end of the year, the "A"s scored much better than the "B"s. In fact, the students had been randomly assigned, so the bias of the teachers (and probably the kids themselves) had profound influence.

This is of course how placebo works. Placebo is an inactive treatment, sometimes called a 'sugar pill'. In fact, placebo may be in a pill or tablet form, or it may be an injection or a medical device. Whatever the form, placebos often look like the real medical treatment that is being studied except they do not contain the active medication. As long as the patient, and better still the doctor, believes in it, it works.

A famous experiment was carried out in 1958 on cardiac patients suffering from angina. This chronic condition, caused by inadequate blood supply in the muscle of the heart wall, often causes severe pain. It was believed at the time that tying off certain arteries in the chest would treat the condition and reduce the pain by allowing new channels to sprout in nearby heart muscle. Some curious (and maybe unscrupulous) surgeons cut open 13 patients with angina and tied their relevant arteries. With another 5 patients with angina, they exposed the arteries but did nothing and just stitched them back up. The surgeons told neither the patients nor their cardiologists which ones were actually operated on.

10 of those who were operated on and all 5 of those who were simply opened, found their angina pain improved significantly, believing it to be due to the relevant surgical procedure. Their conscious experience of pain was reduced because they believed in it. Pathologists later examined the cadavers of patients who had the tie off surgery and found no signs of the newly sprouted blood vessels. We now know that this operation has no physical effect on angina. But their pain did decrease. Because of belief.

We See What We Want to See

"We don't see things as they are; we see them as we are."

- Anaïs Nin, Writer

We may assume that when we look at the world around us, we see it as it is. Everything we experience is shaped at least in part by our social, physical and psychological context.

When you and I look at the same object, we do not always see exactly the same thing. Moreover, when I looked at something at another time and look at it now, even I do not always have the same experience.

We see what we want to see. Let me try and show you what I mean with a clever study that created desire in the innocent participants and tested the consequences on their perceptual experience.

Balcetis and Dunning, two American social psychologists, told participants that the computer would present an image that would determine what they would do next. Some participants were told that if the computer presented an image of a farm animal, they would get to judge a singing competition. If, on the other hand, the computer presented a marine animal, they would have to sing a karaoke tune on the spot in front of judges and a camera. To make the latter even more undesirable and embarrassing, participants watched a

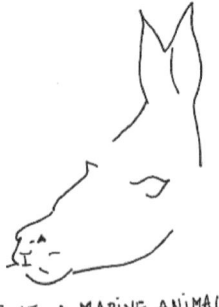

IS IT A MARINE ANIMAL?
IS IT A FARM ANIMAL?

video of a man awkwardly singing off-key and dancing out of step to Gloria Gaynor's 'I Will Survive'. This created the desire to avoid the embarrassment this previous participant seemed to suffer, and increased the desire to see a farm animal. As in many such experiments, for other participants the pairings were switched, where being shown the marine animals was associated with getting the desirable role of judge. The computer then showed participants, for one second, an ambiguous drawing that could be interpreted in one of two ways – as either the head of a donkey or the body of a seal (see above).

Of participants who wished for farm animals, 97 per cent interpreted the drawing as a donkey or horse; however, participants who wished for marine animals were significantly less likely to interpret it as a horse. Participants' wishes affected their perceptual interpretations.

Wishes, hopes, and desires affect what we see quickly and without our awareness. Basically, we perceive the world the way we want it to be.

Coins appears bigger to the poor and powerless. People who have just been socially rejected are better at recognising real smiles and sorting them from fake ones. People most motivated to make it to a finish line or to trudge up a hill actually see the environment as less extreme and the finish line distance as less than those who don't care about getting there. Desires change our perception.

Even how much energy we have affects perception. Joggers estimate that a hill is steeper after finishing a long run compared to estimates made before going out for a run. Older participants perceive the slant of steep hills as greater than younger participants. People with low blood sugar see a hill as steeper than those who just drank a Coke and had their energy fortified.

The way we see things is not some concrete, immutable reality - it's shaped and influenced by our expectations, physical condition, desires, context, etc.

I Know Why I Feel the Way I Do.... Or Do I?

But it gets even more interesting and complicated. Not only do we sometimes not realize that we see what we want to see, we sometimes mistake what is making us feel the way we do. (For those of you that might be interested, that is called Misattribution of Arousal in psychology).

The Misconception: You always know why you feel the way you feel.
The Truth: You can experience emotional states without knowing why, even if you believe you can pinpoint the source of those states.

For example, when actually experiencing physiological responses related to fear, people sometimes mislabel those responses as romantic arousal.
In 1974, psychologists Donald Dutton and Art Aron hired an attractive woman to stand in the middle of a long and scary suspension bridge in British Columbia perched two-hundred and thirty feet above roaring water below. Crossing it would produce terror in anyone.

As men passed her on their way across the bridge, the woman asked them to fill out a questionnaire. At the end of which she asked them to look at an illustration of a lady covering her face and asked them to make up a story of what had just happened to her. Then she told each of the participants that she would be more than happy to discuss the study further if he wanted to call her that evening and tore off a portion of the paper, wrote her number down and handed to each of them.

They then ran the experiment on another bridge, one which would not produce anxiety, a wide sturdy wooden bridge just a few feet off the ground.

50% of the men on the dangerous suspension bridge picked up the phone to call the lady and only 12.5% of those on the safe bridge did so. In addition, the men on the scary bridge were almost twice as likely to come up with a sexually suggestive narrative on the woman story than those on the safe bridge.

It's not that the bridge made the men friskier, but that sometimes we can falsely identify the source of our arousal. In other words, the fear they felt was misinterpreted as sexual arousal. My heart was pounding – did she make me feel that way? Moral of the story: if you want a successful date, choose venues such as roller-coasters, bungee jumps, scuba diving, rock climbing, horror movies rather than candle lit dinners!

It seems that when we feel aroused, we naturally look for context, for an explanation as to why we feel so alive, and this happens automatically and unconsciously. Seldom do we question what we come up with as we don't even realize we are doing this. After we have a Red Bull, an action movie seems even more exciting than if we had just come off a 10-day detox.

Many times, we either don't know or fail to notice what caused us to be physiologically aroused, and we mistakenly attribute the source to something around us, usually other people. And this is true of many emotions. When we are angry, anger will find a host. When we are anxious or fearful, we will find a reason.

Not only have fear and anxiety been researched in this regard, but many other emotions as well.

Psychologist Fritz Strack devised a simple experiment in 1988 where he had folks either hold a pen between their teeth with an open mouth or between their closed lips as they read cartoon strips. They tended to rate the cartoons as funnier when they held the pen between their teeth than between their lips. Between the teeth, some of the same muscles used for smiling were contracted. While between the lips, those of a frown were used. Their bodies gave them feedback on how to feel.

As one of the founders of psychology, Willian James, once said...

"Act your way into a feeling".

The source of our emotional states is often hard or impossible to detect. If you feel something and you don't know why, you often tend to pin it on a target, usually another person who fits the narrative you are about to spin in your head. Remember sometimes that target could be yourself. We keep searching for the reason because we think of ourselves like scientists. In fact, we are much more like the lawyer...we know the answer (we are feeling the sensation we usually associate with being angry) and then we find the evidence to justify that feeling (we settle on something – the noisy person beside us, the food I just ate). It feels good to assume that we have found the source of our feeling, be it anger, happiness, anxiety, whatever. I remember how during my menopause when my body was feeling tense, was overwhelmed with hot flushes and it gave me all the cues of anxiety and stress, I blamed my emotions on external factors, such as work colleagues or friends, when in fact the physical cues were a result of my hormonal changes.

7.
LIVE EACH DAY LIKE A GROUNDHOG DAY -TIME IS OUR MOST VALUABLE RESOURCE

"It is not that we have a short time to live, but that we waste a lot of it."

— Seneca, *On the Shortness of Life*

Meet Joe Blogs. He spends 8 to 9 hours a day working at a computer. He spends about another 2 and a half hours a day on social media. He is constantly busy. At weekends, while he often has plans to practice piano or exercise, he invariably gets distracted. He gets bored easily and when there is a hint of boredom, he checks Instagram for any likes or comments, checks his WhatsApp, checks anything really. Joe has been planning on going back to college for years to do a one-year course to work with elderly people. He hasn't gotten around to it yet. Things keep cropping up – not enough time, not enough money.

If you are anything like Joe, read on.

How We Spend Our Time
"How we spend our days is, of course, how we spend our lives."

- Annie Dillard, Author

The original idea for the 1993 movie *Groundhog Day* came from a book by German philosopher Friedrich Nietzsche where the writer describes a man living the same day over and over. With Groundhog Day in mind, we may ask ourselves how do we really spend our days?

If we calculated our time with such care and precision as we do our money, we may waste less. And money can be replaced, whereas time cannot.

Perception of time and how we use it is a tricky thing. What if our lives were reshuffled into a new order where all the moments that share a quality were magically grouped together? With a probing imagination and deep understanding of the human condition, acclaimed neuroscientist David Eagleman did just that in his "Sum: Forty Tales from the Afterlives".

"You spend two months driving the street in front of your house, seven months having sex. For five months straight you flip through magazines while sitting on a toilet. You spend six days clipping your nails. Fifteen months looking for lost items. Two years of boredom: staring out a bus window, sitting in an airport terminal. One year reading books.

Two weeks wondering what happens when you die. Six weeks waiting for a green light. Four weeks sitting in thought, wondering if there is something better you could be doing with your time. Four minutes wondering what your life would be like if you reshuffled the order of events."

- David Eagleman, *Sum: Forty Tales From The Afterlife*

Thankfully we don't live our lives this way, squashing the time we do one activity into one block. Eagleman reiterated how the particular linear quality of events through which we live our lives is precisely what makes our lives not only tolerable but thrilling. And in so doing, his clever thought experiment jolts us out of our hubris and complacency about "almost living" - forever.

Philosophers Have Pondered How We Use Time for Millennia

"Life can only be understood backwards; but it must be lived forwards."

- Kierkegaard

"Life is short so use it well" was my mother's mantra. What if we listened to Kierkegaard, and attempt to understand how we use the time of our lives "forward", i.e. before we run out of time.

The upsetting reckoning of time wasted versus time meaningfully spent may seem like a modern problem, but while the nature of technology and gadgets has undeniably exacerbated the ratio, the equation itself stretches all the way to antiquity, with only the variables altered. The equation of how to balance our time more favourably toward a life of presence and good rather than one of waste and want, is what many philosophers have examined - from the first-century Roman philosopher Seneca in "Letters from a Stoic", to Walt Whitman's contemplation on what makes life worth living in "Specimen Day". More recently Oliver Burkeman, British author, wrote "Four Thousand Weeks" (what the average person gets on this planet) on how to make the most of it.

In the same way as we reason how best to spend a limited budget of money, we can consider how best to spend our limited time on this planet.

Many of us slide through life in a trance of expectancy, always running from the present moment in order to get to the next - a process which of course ends with death.

"What man can you show me who places any value on his time, who reckons the worth of each day, who understands that he is dying daily? Therefore... hold every hour in your grasp. Lay hold of to-day's task, and you will not need to depend so much upon tomorrow's. While we are postponing, life speeds by. Nothing... is ours, except time."

- Seneca

Prioritize, Prioritize, Prioritize

"The key is not to prioritize what's on your schedule, but to schedule your priorities".

Stephen Covey, *Seven Habits of Highly Effective People*

We don't usually think about our lives as a collection of hours but as a collage of meaningful moments. Think about things that are meaningful to you. The smallest moments can have the biggest impact on your life. During her journey through Wonderland, Alice asks the White Rabbit, "How long is forever?" And the White Rabbit replies: *"Sometimes, just one second."*

"Let us reflect on what is truly of value in life, what gives meaning to our lives, and set our priorities on the basis of that."

- The Dalai Lama

Give It a Try: Determine Your Priorities

How do I spend my time? – do I spend enough on health? On friends? On my partner? On career?

Using Covey's excellent Time Management Grid (also known as the Eisenhower matrix), fill in some examples of how you spend your time. Then note what you can carve away that is a waste of your time.

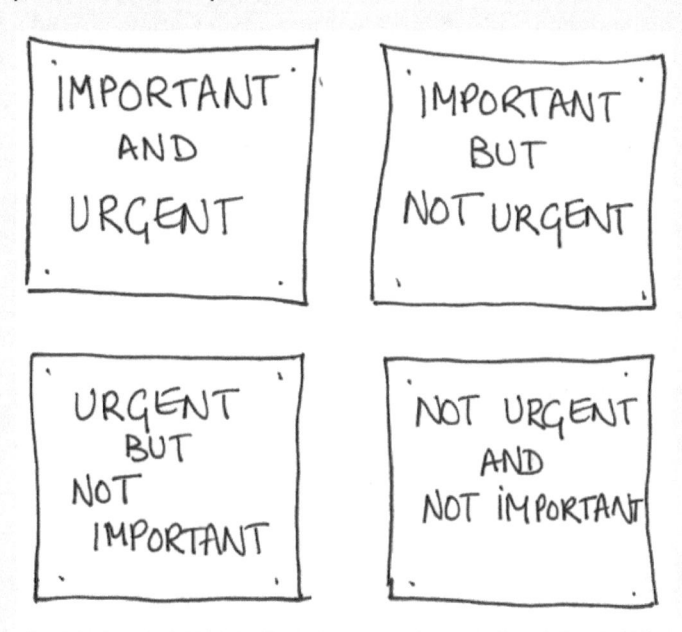

IMPORTANT AND URGENT	IMPORTANT BUT NOT URGENT
URGENT BUT NOT IMPORTANT	NOT URGENT AND NOT IMPORTANT

The Urgent/Not Important and Not Urgent/Not Important activities are where we waste time.

Ask yourself –
Do I have to have to do it today?
Do I have to do it now?
Do I have to do it at all?

The Urgent/Not Important activities (such as responding to things that look like crises like some emails and phone calls) is where stress builds up – unnecessarily. The impact of this can be reduced by paying more attention to the Important/Not Urgent sector which includes things like planning, developing resilience, meeting friends, quality time with family etc.

This activity is a good way of focusing the lens on how exactly the hours dwindle away.

What Do You Do on a Daily Basis?
Remember that a life is merely a day repeated.

Give It a Try: Daily Reconstruction

Try 2 things:
Watch and note the aftertaste of the things you do, the people you meet; almost like counting calories, except for emotions, not food. Keep a record of how present you are while doing those things. Stop measuring days by degree of productivity and start experiencing them by degree of presence.

Fill in the grid below for every day this week and note the following at the end of each day. What were you doing and who were you with when you were at your best and worst? What activities made happy/ unhappy/stressed?

EVENT NAME — WHAT WERE YOU DOING + WITH WHOM?	BEGAN	ENDED	WHAT DID YOU FEEL?
eg. PADDLE BOARD YOGA - WITH FRIENDS	10.30 AM	12.00	UPLIFTED

The Power of Now

"One day you will wake up and there won't be any more time to do the things you've always wanted. Do it now."

- Paulo Coelho, *The Witch of Portobello, a novel.*

We don't need to look to Joe Blogs for an example of procrastination. Now really is the only time we have. And when we think of tomorrow or next year, when we get there we will be in the Now as well. Now is all we have. So use it.

Give It a Try: What is Important to You?

Draw 4 circles and write what is important to you and what you want for yourself – a circle for each timeframe - today, this month, this year, your life.

What is worth spending a lot of time on for you?

What would a good life look like to you and what will you do today to start creating it? Create your own Groundhog Day.

When I wrote this chapter, I calculated that if I live an average lifespan, I have about another 1000 weeks left!

A little reminder – if you are 40 years old and reading this, you have on average 13,500 days left in your life, that is 1,930 weeks approximately! Use them well.

FORGET BUSYNESS... ALLOW BOREDOM

"How you been?... Busy.
How's work?... Busy.
How was your week?... Good. Busy.
You name the question, busy is the answer. Yes, yes, I know, we are all terribly busy doing terribly important things. But I think more often than not, busy is simply the most acceptable knee-jerk response.

Yet busy stands alone as the easiest way of summarizing all that you do and all that you are.
"I am busy" is the short way of saying -- implying -- "My time is filled, my phone does not stop ringing and you (therefore) should think well of me.""

- Amy Krouse Rosenthal, Sweet Nothing

In today's digital world, many of us are constantly on the go - manically juggling emails, social media, and never-ending to-do lists. We may feel that we thrive on being busy, getting a buzz out of hyperactive multi-tasking. We live in an anxiety-drenched, productivity-obsessed age.

Busyness has become a status symbol. Contemporary Westerners praise being overworked. They see busy individuals as possessing rare and desirable characteristics, such as competence and ambition. As we saw above, we spend hours of our lives on the phone, watching commercials, waiting in line, etc. But is this obsession with relentless activity giving us space to really think and reflect on the important stuff?

So why do we do it? Because we don't want to be bored. Ever. Flicking mindlessly through Apps or newsfeeds seems far better than even a moment of boredom.

From Kierkegaard bemoaning the absurdity of busyness to Emerson's observation that "our hurry and embarrassment look ridiculous", the philosophers noted that our addiction to busyness is our attempt to escape from ourselves. Indeed, Kierkegaard recommended boredom as opportune moments for imaginative reflection. For example, someone might choose to be entertained by the monotonous sound of water dripping from a roof. His solution to boredom is akin to what we now call mindfulness training.

Studies show boredom makes us more creative and productive. Giving our minds space is a lot more valuable than we might realise.

The reality is that time spent being busy is not always productive or meaningful. Constant busyness poses a threat to our mental health in the long-term. While giving the illusion of control, it can become a manic defence mechanism, blocking negative thoughts and feelings. Frantically dealing with different tasks enables us to temporarily suppress the demons of loneliness, anxiety and depression. However, not dealing with what is really troubling us eventually leads to burnout.

Have you ever been furiously focused on a problem for a long time, unable to solve it, until you leave it aside and - miraculously - have a 'Eureka!' moment when you're thinking about something completely different? It's no coincidence that many artists, scientists and mathematicians have had brilliant ideas while in the bath or lying in bed. So give it a try.

Give It a Try: Get Bored

The likes of Google, Pixar and Facebook have incorporated disconnected time, or contemplative practices such as meditation, as part of their working culture. At first glance, it may seem counterintuitive for an employee to encourage their workers to *stop* working- to disconnect from the very technology they are responsible for developing or selling! But what's going on here is that research shows that taking mindful breaks during work hours is of sufficient benefit to their employees to up their productivity and creativity.

So, go ahead, STOP. Forget being uncomfortable with the guilt associated with doing nothing. Push unimportant tasks away, leave time to think creatively – without having any set agenda to do so. Turn off the phone. For an hour, a day, days. Allow yourself periods of nothingness.

8. CULTIVATE SOCIAL CONNECTIONS

"In a world of algorithms hashtags and followers, know the true importance of human connection."

- Simi Fromen, Author

Meet Social Isolate. He works a lot and spends any free time he has on social media. He has little time for making social connections and relied on his wife for company. Since his wife left him, he is intensely lonely. His mental and physical health has suffered since she left. He never thought he needed others. But now he does. Where and how is he going to meet people and if and when he does, how to be with them?

We are social creatures. As far back as we can trace, humans have travelled, hunted, and thrived in social groups and for good reason. Humans who were separated from their tribe often suffered severe consequences. And nothing has changed.

Social connections have been consistently found to enhance our happiness. In fact, having a rich social network points to a number of mental health benefits, such as increased feelings of belonging, purpose, increased levels of happiness, improved self-worth and confidence, less stress-related illnesses and a lower risk of mental illness.

Strong social ties are important to our sense of identity and importantly, are not subject to that pesky human tendency to tire of things that once brought us happiness. In other words, it's not like me with my delight in my new job when I knew that sooner or later the novelty would wear off. Having friends and social connections is not prone to hedonic adaptation.

Social connectedness is critical for good health. People with limited social connectedness have poorer mental and physical health, including increased depression, and die earlier than those with strong social connectedness. You might ask which is the egg and which is the chicken? Do social connections lead to better psychological health or does poor psychological health lead to reduced social connectedness?

A 20-year longitudinal study in New Zealand on nearly 22,000 people found social connectedness to be a stronger and more consistent predictor of mental health year-on-year than mental health was of social connectedness. In other words, it is our social connections that lead to better mental health rather than the other way around. Social connectedness is often referred to as a form of *capital* that an individual can draw upon in times of need, and which will protect their mental health.

Social connections not only impact our mental health, but our physical health as well. A robust body of scientific evidence has indicated that lack of social connection is a greater determinant of poor health than obesity, smoking, or high blood pressure. Strong social connections can actually improve our immune systems.

Social connections even help us to live longer. A prospective study carried out by a team at Stanford University School of Medicine confirmed that support groups not only improved quality of life, reduced distress, anxiety and pain but also gave a survival benefit for a subgroup of participants with an aggressive form of breast cancer. Following the breast cancer patients for periods of up to 10 years, they found that those women who were randomly assigned to a support group where they met with other women who had survived cancer on a weekly basis survived on average a year longer than others who received educational materials.

Other studies have confirmed this connection between social connection and longevity. A review of 148 studies (308,849 participants) indicated that the individuals with stronger social relationships had a 50% increased likelihood of survival. This remained true across a number of factors, including age, sex, initial health status, and cause of death.

With loneliness on the rise, it is more important than ever to invest in human connection. By neglecting our need to connect, we put our health at risk.

We Are Not in This Alone - 3 Degrees of Separation

My neighbour is always pleasant and happy. And when I meet her, I feel good afterwards and then later when I go to my local café I smile at the waitress. Could it be possible that my pleasant neighbour infected the waitress indirectly with her smile? Seems so.

An interesting phenomenon with social connections is that happiness is "infectious". It spreads through social networks like an emotional contagion. Researchers from Harvard Medical School looked at the happiness levels of nearly 5000 individuals over a period of 20 years and found that happiness undergoes "3 degrees of separation"; when an individual becomes happy, the network effect can be measured up to three degrees. One person's happiness triggers a chain reaction that benefits not only his friends, but his friends' friends, and his friends' friends' friends. And the effect lasts for up to one year. Conversely (and thankfully, if you ask me), sadness does not spread through social networks as robustly as happiness. Despite the old adage, it is happiness which appears to like company more so than misery.

While an individual becoming happy increases his friend's chances of happiness (by up to 34%), a friend of that friend experiences a nearly 10 percent chance of increased happiness, and a friend of that friend has a 5.6 percent increased chance— a three-degree cascade.

As an interesting aside, this is the third major network analysis by the same Harvard researchers (Nicholas Christakis and James Fowler) that shows how our health is affected by our social context. The two previous studies described the social network effects in obesity and smoking cessation. I recall when I lived in the remote outback of northern Western Australia, obesity was the norm as was type 2 diabetes. Folks told me that once they moved there, they often just "let themselves go"! Poor health behaviours may also be contagious, it seems.

Are Social Media Connections Just as Good as Real Life Relationships?

Facebook's mission "to make the world more open and connected" is a familiar refrain among company leaders. But research shows connecting 2.9 billion users through the internet may come at a psychological cost.

Nowadays, although most of us are well aware that self-representations on Instagram or Facebook are illusory, we nevertheless feel pressured to engage in this competition, sharing our achievements and experiences over social media to show others how we are keeping up.

This fuels a perpetual competition, focused on the sharing of successes and other updates, regardless of how accurately these portrayals represent real life — and they rarely do.

Research provides mixed clues about how social media use influences our subjective well-being. Some research reveals negative associations between online social network use (in particular Facebook) and well-being, while others reveal the opposite. Still other work suggests that the relationship between Facebook use and well-being may be more nuanced and potentially influenced by multiple factors including number of Facebook friends, perceived supportiveness of one's online network, depressive symptomatology, loneliness, and self-esteem.

A study conducted by the University of Michigan, suggests that the more people used Facebook, the worse they felt and increased Facebook usage contributes to anxiety and even depression. By constantly seeing what others are doing, and in paying attention to their lives as they seem to be unfolding in real-time, our anxiety and uncertainty as to whether we are leading lives that fulfil our own potential deepens. Overall, this sharing and social comparison has psychological consequences. One solution if you're feeling fed-up and lonely: the prescription for Facebook despair is... less Facebook. The researchers found that face-to-face or phone interaction — those outmoded, analogue ways of communication — had the opposite effect. Direct interactions with other human beings led people to feel better.

"We humans are social beings. We come into the world as the result of others' actions. We survive here in dependence on others. Whether we like it or not, there is hardly a moment of our lives when we do not benefit from others' activities. For this reason, it is hardly surprising that most of our happiness arises in the context of our relationships with others."

-The Dalai Lama

Give It a Try: Invest in Social Connections

Our inherent need for human connection doesn't mean that every introvert must become a social butterfly. Having human connection can look different for each person.

Meet a friend, call them, text them. Tell them why you appreciate them. Be specific, that always works better than a general note of thanks and appreciation.

Devote time to becoming active in your community - volunteer, join a club or organization.

If you meet a potential friend, create an opportunity to spend time together.

Reach out to an old friend you've lost touch with.

Eat lunch in a communal space.

Introduce yourself to your neighbours.

Ask someone for help when you need it.

Remember that social connections impact your overall health and well-being and they require time and effort.

LOSSES LOOM LARGER THAN GAINS ...
MINE, MINE, MINE!

"Some studies have estimated that losses have more than twice the psychological impact as equivalent gains. The fact is, we all hate to lose."

- Barry Schwartz, Psychologist

Money to Burn
"Money is acting like a drug, not chemically but psychologically."

- Claudia Hammond,
Mind Over Money: The Psychology of Money and How to Use It Better

A couple of years ago when I was giving talks on which this book is based, I tore up five 50$ bills before the audience. Literally, people in the audience were enraged, stood up and asked what was going on. But of course, I had copied the $ bills and was a distance from them so they couldn't tell. It wasn't even their money!

Now imagine seeing a million crisp 50-dollar notes (real ones this time) going up in flames in a bonfire in a disused boathouse on the Scottish island of Jura. How would you feel? Probably nothing short of rampant horror and fury, right? Well, that's exactly what British art duo the K Foundation did in 1994: they put one million pounds on fire. The motivation behind their action was to perform a conceptual art piece. People responded to the YouTube of the event with anger and severe criticism— could they not have used the money to buy food for the hungry or houses for the homeless? How could they have been so selfish? Of course, if they had used it on drugs or cars, no one would have noticed. The key message here is: Money evokes strong feelings in all of us.

According to one of the art duo's members, they hadn't actually destroyed anything real. They simply burned a pile of paper rather than, say, bread. And therein lies the intrinsic contradiction of money. In a way, they were right. Paper money in itself is valueless – or at least it would be if you lived on a desert island where there was nothing to buy. But in reality, money is a tool and its destruction is a destruction of opportunities. $¥£€ are SYMBOLIC. Just as when we are given a reward like chocolate, when we are given money, the reward centre of brain lights up, as it represents opportunity later.

Our brains learn quickly when it comes to financial losses.

We all know the feeling. How many times have you come home from a long day at work or returned from a holiday only to find a stack of bills waiting for you in the mailbox? The moment you see those letters you're filled with dread. Similarly, many people can't help but think the worst whenever they receive an unexpected call from their accountant or the tax office.

Research done at the National Research University Higher School of Economics, Moscow, found that when an individual experiences a financial loss (even just an overdue water bill), the brain takes note and remembers to react strongly to similar future events. Just as learning a second language or mastering a musical instrument sparks changes in how the brain interacts with external stimuli, so also with our response to loss of money. Even if that overdue tax we have to cough up will go to paying for our kids' education or our parents' care!

We Make Judgements in Relative Terms

"The cost of a thing is the amount of what I will call life which is required to be exchanged for it, immediately or in the long run".

- Henry David Thoreau, *Walden*

When I go to buy, let's say, washing up liquid, invariably, there is a very expensive one (super-duper & eco-friendly). There is a very cheap one, probably made by the store, like Aldi or Lidl. And then there is the middle-priced one, which is the one most people buy. "It's not overpriced and not of poor quality" is what our brains invariably believe.

When I go to buy a car, the salesperson will always show me the most expensive one first, and then the middle and lower range - within his available car fleet. He knows that by showing me the expensive one first, he has what psychologists call "anchored" me. Having looked at models well beyond my budget, other, cheaper cars look like a bargain - even if they cost more than I was initially intending to spend. Whether it is a phone, a new house, or a computer, most sales people are in on the "anchoring" trick. And our brains always fall for it. Even when we know that is what is happening.

A couple of years ago, *'The Economist'* magazine came up with its subscription offers. They wanted to provide readers the option of both print and online editions to choose from. And you just can't simply ask customers directly what they would pay. Naturally enough, the company was betting on its readers choosing the second alternative below over the first one.

Which subscription would you choose?
1. Economist online subscription: US59$ (One-year online access to all *The Economist* articles).
2. Print and Web subscription: US125$ (One-year subscription to the print edition of *The Economist* and online access to all articles).

In reality, things turned out to be quite the opposite. More and more customers favoured the first option, while a handful went for the second one.
1. 59$ online only – 68%
2. 125$ print and online – 32%

It didn't take them long to realize that something was wrong with their marketing psychology. So they added a third option. And thereby fooled their customers into paying more.

Which subscription would you choose?
1. Economist online subscription: US59$ (One-year online access to all *The Economist* articles)
2. Print subscription: US$125 (One-year subscription to the print edition of *The Economist*)
3. Print and Web subscription: US125$ (One-year subscription to the print edition of *The Economist* and online access to all articles)

They found that the majority of their customers choose what seemed to their unsuspecting brains the best "bargain". 84% of them choose the print and online version.
1. 59$ online only – 16%
2. 125$ print only – 0%
3. 125$ print and online- 84%

Supposedly, the magazine increased its sales by 43% after this pricing strategy.

Be careful of those mobile phone plans! There will always be 3 to choose from and your brain will invariably be fooled.

We are swayed by context. I will travel across town to get something, such as a child's toy, that costs $50 in the shop near me for $15 less in the place across town. Yet, if I am buying a car, I probably won't bother to do the same if the car costs $10,000 in my local garage, but $9,985 across town. But 15$ is 15$!

We make judgements in relative terms, not absolute terms. We may be happy with our salary, but if we hear the guy at the next desk is getting more, we suddenly become less satisfied.

And then there are "On Sale" signs. We act more quickly and with less thought in considering a purchase if it's "On Sale" than if there is no "Sale" sign.

We generally think expensive means good quality. But not always.

After all that thinking, you may feel like a glass of wine! Psychologists decided to test the extent to which the price tag of a bottle of wine correlates with people's opinion of its quality. They asked 600 people to taste a variety of wines ranging from $5 to $50. They then asked them to guess which wines they thought were the most expensive. The study was double-blinded which means that neither the experimenter nor the tasters knew which wine was which. This is important to make sure there was no bias and that the experimenter was not letting anything away.

They were only able to tell the real expensive wine close to 50% of times. That is to say that flipping a coin would have been equally accurate.

Does this mean then that it is utterly stupid to buy expensive wines and that we would enjoy some cheap plonk just as much? Seems to be so!

Psychologists at California Institute of Technology took 20 people and placed them inside a fMRI scanner that measures brain activity based on changes in blood flowing to the different brain areas. The more active they become, the more blood these areas will require to oxygenate and feed their neurons. Once inside the scanner they were given five different wines priced $5-$90 via a straw (no space for a glass!). In fact, only three were different. The same wine appeared twice, once as a cheap wine and a second time as a pricey one. Subjects couldn't tell the difference between the cheap and expensive ones.

However, when they told them the price of the wines they were tasting, they always said the more expensive wines tasted better, even in those cases when the wine was the same except for the price tag. And when they knew the prices, the part of the frontal cortex related to decision making and integrating thought processes and actions together with internal desires (orbitofrontal cortex) got more active; adding the value of the wine's price to the sensation perceived by both the nose and mouth.

In other words, our brains believe the price tag!

Paying Cash Causes Pain in our Brains

When have you paid for things on holidays with a credit card, and found that you forgot or underestimated what you spent? When we pay a tip with a credit card, we give a bigger one than if we use cash. It is easier to pay with a credit card, because for most of us, paying with cash is actually painful for our brains.

An Italian study looked at the neural correlates of payment methods – cash, card or smartphone for different amounts of money (10E, 50E or 150E). They found greater activation of the emotional parts of the brain when making a cash payment than either the card or smartphone, with any amount of money. And an even greater activation was observed with 150E than 50E or 10E, only in the cash condition. In other words, paying by cash hurts!

As paying by cash could be a more effective way for us to 'feel' the loss of spending, it might be best to leave aside the card and smartphone if you are prone to compulsive shopping or digital gambling!

Loses Loom Larger than Gains

We care more about losing a dollar than gaining a dollar. The famous dictum from Israeli psychologists, Daniel Kahneman and Amos Tversky that *losses loom larger than gains* implies that people impute greater value to a given item when they give it up than when they acquire it. We fear loss more than we welcome gains.

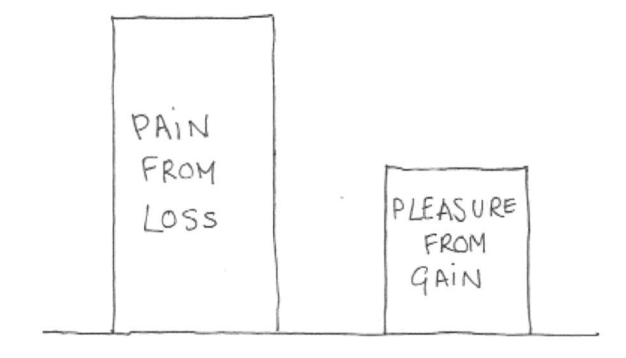

So, what causes us to be more sensitive to losses? In 1979 psychologists Tversky and Kahneman developed a successful behavioural model, called prospect theory, using the principles of loss aversion, to explain how people assess uncertainty. More recently, psychologists and neuroscientists have uncovered how loss aversion may work on a neural level. In 2007 psychologists at University of California Los Angeles found that the brain regions that process value and reward may be silenced more when we evaluate a potential loss than they are activated when we assess a similar-sized gain. They also found that different individuals displayed varying degrees of sensitivity to loss aversion, and these wide-ranging neural responses predicted differences in their behaviour. For instance, people with stronger neural sensitivity to both losses and gains were more risk-averse.

We are bombarded on a daily basis with loss aversion marketing tactics whether we realize it or not. "Only 3 left in stock! Order now!" "Available while supplies last" "Flash Sale! Today Only!" Our aversion to loss, even when we know that is how our brain works, causes us fear of missing out on what appears to be a good deal. We are all likely to be taken in by this strategy even when we know about it!

The Endowment Effect

"Once something is given to you, it's yours. Once it becomes part of your endowment, even after a very few minutes, giving it up will entail a loss."

- Barry Schwartz, Psychologist, *The Paradox of Choice: Why More Is Less*

We ascribe more value to things merely because we own them. This is what behavioural psychologists call the endowment effect. It is the tendency of people to value an object that they own more highly than they would value the same object if it didn't belong to them. I tend to expect my house to be priced more highly than its true fair-market value. Yet, I equally expect that the house I am buying should be cheaper than it is (that is, until I own it!). The endowment effect is also sometimes referred to as the "ownership effect." And the longer I own something, the more I value it and don't want to part with it.

This could be due to the general phenomenon of loss aversion, which means that we give possible losses more weight than potential gains of the same magnitude. It could also be due to psychological inertia, i.e. we prefer not to change the status quo of our lives unless it really matters. It could also be due to the fact that once a thing is "mine", it is part of my identity and I don't want to lose it.

Take Home Messages:
- Don't let your brain be fooled by Sale signs, anchoring prices, etc.
    - Ignore Relative Comparisons. For example, on a menu, you may see a high price at the top, and then everything else seems cheap.
    - Pay attention to what something costs, not how big a discount you're getting.
    - Remember the salesperson is using Anchoring – the first number mentioned in a given scenario unconsciously influences our future choices. For example, if you are buying a car, its likely you will be first shown cars with a high price in order to influence the offer you make. Have an informed 'anchor' in advance, then it's harder to be influenced.
    - If bargaining, do your research in advance.

- Focus on what you actually want and on what is of value to you. Don't get caught up in whether the item is priced fairly or not, consider its value to YOU. For example, do I book a flight leaving in the middle of the night because it is $50 cheaper, even though I know I will be exhausted the next day? Do I get an Uber on a rainy night instead of walking home?

- If you are selling something, imagine you don't own it.

- If you have experienced financial losses and react with dread to those window envelopes (i.e. bills), try to retrain your brain to be less stressed by remembering financial gains, times when you were perhaps overpaid for something, or how much you have, rather than what you don't have. Refer to the numbers, not the feelings.

- The source of where we get money affects how we use it. For example, if I get a bonus, or win some money at the casino or get some tax back, I may well think of this as extra and may be more likely to spend it on frivolous things. Serious money is the salary, but money is money!

- If you tend to overspend, then make spending painful. Use cash rather than your credit card or smartphone. When we use our credit card or phone, we are more likely to underestimate what we spend.

9.
KINDNESS AND COMPASSION

"Practice kindness all day to everybody and you will realize you're already in heaven now. Commit to being kind to someone today."

- Jack Kerouac

When I asked my mother just a few days before her death at 88, what was the best thing she learnt from her mother, she thought for a moment and said - kindness. To treat everyone with kindness.

"Three things in human life are important – to be kind, to be kind, to be kind"

- William James, Father of Psychology

Philosophers, writers, religious figures, and now researchers as well, offer an abiding answer to a healthy and happy life – commit to kindness, kind thoughts and kind actions. The meaning of kindness fundamentally refers to being open-hearted, when I give of myself without expecting anything in return.

Research shows that kindness benefits not only the receiver but also the giver. Whether you are recipient or giver or merely just a witness you can feel the benefits of an increase in oxytocin, commonly called the "love hormone". This helps to lower blood pressure, improve overall heart-health, increase self-esteem and optimism. It can decrease pain by generating endorphins (the brain's natural painkiller). Kindness can increase the feeling of strength and energy due to helping others.

Practising kindness can help us feel calmer, less stressed and more positive. It can even help with depression and anxiety. A team at the University of British Columbia did a study on a group of highly anxious individuals in which they performed at least 6 acts of kindness a week. After one month, there was a significant increase in positive moods, relationship satisfaction and a decrease in social avoidance in socially anxious individuals.

Preliminary neuroendocrine (hormonal) studies show that Loving Kindness Meditation may decrease stress-induced subjective suffering and immune response.

Older adults who stay active by volunteering are getting more out of it than just an altruistic feeling - they are receiving a health boost too, researchers report. Volunteering is associated with reductions in symptoms of depression, better overall health, fewer functional limitations, and greater longevity. This is a stronger effect than exercising four times a week or going to church.

"My religion is simple. My religion is kindness."

- The Dalai Lama

Giving Up on Kindness

We are often afraid to be kind in case of having too high a cost to pay or for fear of our vulnerability being exploited. Unfortunately, we live in an age where cynicism and self-protection can easily become our flawed self-defence mechanisms which we use against the perceived risks of kindness to others.

Kindness is sometimes viewed with suspicion: it is either a form of selfishness (and ultimately secretly exploitative…as when the rich give donations to charity to evade tax), or a way to win approval. Independence and self-reliance have become the yardstick of success.

In many ways, we have a paradoxical relationship with kindness. On the one hand, we may be somewhat suspicious of it, we often deny our kind impulses, we may jeer those who are over-kind as being hopeless and yet we are outraged when people are unkind to us. On the other hand, we are unwilling to live a life guided by kindness, but desperately crave others to be kind to us.

A friend adopted a Korean child in Japan when he was about 4. He had spent his life until then in an orphanage, where he shared everything with the other children. When he would share and often give his toys to others who liked them, his mom would advise against it, stressing the fact to him that they were *his* toys. Maybe all children are naturally kind, and with contemporary society's focus on independence and resourcefulness, they seem to grow out of it.

We are all vulnerable at every stage of life. We all live with uncertainty. Uncertainty of illness, accident, economic tragedy, etc. Our vulnerability is what we have in common. In fact, *"vulnerability is the core, the heart, the centre of meaningful human experiences"*, according to Brené Brown, a professor and vulnerability researcher at the University of Houston. Real kindness has unpredictable consequences and may leave us vulnerable. Learning to feel comfortable with the risk of making ourselves vulnerable enough to be kind is an important lesson.

Give It a Try: Nurture Kindness

Give. Giving is therapeutic. Giving time, service, care, kind thoughts, words. Give an unexpected gift. Send silent love to the guy at the gas station who filled your car. Let others go ahead of you in a queue or in traffic.

Smile genuinely at 5 strangers throughout your day.

Each time you meet a friend, or when you have to have a meeting with your boss, or indeed when you meet anyone, consciously imagine filling a space between you and them by putting kindness there.

Give others the benefit of the doubt.

When your thoughts go negative towards someone, remind yourself of their good qualities or sometime when they did something good and kind, and focus your mind on the positive aspects. Train your brain to think kind thoughts.

"Kindness enriches our life; with kindness mysterious things become clear, difficult things become easy, and dull things become cheerful. Nothing can make our life, or the lives of other people, more beautiful than perpetual kindness."

- Tolstoy

And remember receiving kindness is as important as giving. I remember when my mother told my nephew who had enthusiastically given her a gift from his travels to China, that he shouldn't have wasted his money on her. He was deflated. Cherish what is given to you.

Compassion

"If you want others to be happy, practice compassion. If you want to be happy, practice compassion."

-The Dalai Lama

Those who regularly practice loving kindness meditation are able to increase their capacity for forgiveness, connection to others and their self-acceptance.

Give It a Try:
Practice Compassion, Loving Kindness /Metta Meditation

Carve out some quiet time for yourself (even a few minutes will work) and sit comfortably. Close your eyes, relax your muscles, and take a few deep breaths.

Scan your body and completely relax each part. Note how peaceful you feel. Cultivate inner peace.

Imagine a little kitten or a child, someone or something that naturally generates a feeling of love in your heart. Focus on this feeling of love for the kitten, child or person. Imagine that you are breathing out tension and breathing in feelings of love.

Repeat three or four positive, reassuring phrases to your object of love and compassion. These messages are examples, but you can also create your own:

May you be happy and safe
May you always be healthy, peaceful, and strong

Bask in feelings of warmth and compassion for a few moments. If your attention drifts, gently redirect it back to these feelings of loving kindness. Let these feelings envelop you.

You can choose to either stay with this focus for the duration of your meditation or begin to shift your focus to loved ones in your life. Begin with someone who you are very close to, such as a spouse, a child, a parent, or a best friend. Feel your gratitude and love for them. Stay with that feeling. You may want to repeat the reassuring phrases.

Once you've held these feelings toward that person, bring other important people from your life into your awareness, one by one, and envision them with perfect wellness and inner peace. Then branch out to other friends, family members, neighbours, and acquaintances.

> Extend feelings of loving kindness to people around the globe and focus on a feeling of connection and compassion. You may even want to include those with whom you are in conflict to help reach a place of forgiveness or greater peace.
>
> Now bring the loving kindness back to yourself. Imagine feeling perfect love for yourself, thanking yourself for all that you are, knowing that you are just right—just as you are. Breathe in "love", breathe out "let go".
>
> Repeat three or four positive, reassuring phrases to yourself. These messages are examples, but you can also create your own:
>
> May I be happy
> May I be safe
> May I be healthy, peaceful, and strong
> May I give and receive appreciation today
>
> When you feel that your meditation is complete, open your eyes. Remember that you can revisit the wonderful feelings you generated throughout the day. Internalize how loving kindness meditation feels, and return to those feelings by shifting your focus and taking a few deep breaths.

There are lots of recordings of Loving Kindness Meditation on the internet, e.g. https://www.youtube.com/watch?v=sz7cpV7ERsM
Have a look to see what suits you.

Being Kind to Oneself

It is important to be kind to oneself. In fact, there is a growing area of psychology called Self-compassion, pioneered by Kristin Neff, an associate professor in the University of Texas, who has written a number of books on the topic, including "Self-Compassion, Step By Step: The Proven Power of Being Kind to Yourself".

Become aware of when you criticize yourself for something that has happened, such as forgetting where you put something, or said something you didn't mean to. Take time to acknowledge and observe your self-critical voice and reframe its observations in a friendlier way; you will eventually form the blueprint for changing how you relate to yourself long-term.

The habit of practicing kindness towards oneself naturally spills out into our dealings with others – an overall boost to the balance of kindness in the world.

Treat yourself to a massage.

Delight in Others' Happiness – *Mudita* in the Age of Envy

My mother was always delighted to hear the good news or good fortune of others. I remember she used to say "the blessing of God in them" and she would rub her hands together in glee as if the good fortune had been her own. People loved to tell my mother their good news. She was actively thrilled for them. This quality is rare. It is a gladness at others' happiness that is flooded with respect, and it is limitless. It is what the Buddhists call *"mudita"*. It is defined as *"sympathetic, vicarious joy; happiness rather than resentment at someone else's well-being or good fortune; the opposite of schadenfreude."* In the English language, there isn't a word that translates to mean the same. The word *schadenfreude*, which is of German origin and the opposite of *mudita*, translates to mean taking pleasure in the misfortune of others.

Many years ago, I had a series of disappointments. I didn't get the scholarship I had applied for. My visa to work in Australia was declined. A paper I had written was refused publication. I remember how a friend of mine delighted at my misfortune; she had a feeling of schadenfreude. She always took active delight when friends' lives were not working out for them, feeling somehow that if they were more unhappy, she would be happier. Maybe you know someone like her. Someone who always seems to be happier when others are unhappy. We often censor what we tell these folks when things are going well for us and we are happy. Human beings have always felt what Aristotle defined in the fourth century BC as pain at the sight of another's good fortune.

Stephen Covey coined the term "abundance mentality" in his best-selling book, "The 7 Habits of Highly Effective People". It is a lot like *mudita*. Its opposite, "scarcity mentality", which describes the friend I mentioned above, refers to people seeing life as a finite pie, so that if one person takes a big piece, that leaves less for everyone else.

"Have an abundance mentality: When people are genuinely happy at the successes of others, the pie gets larger.

People with a Scarcity Mentality have a very hard time being genuinely happy for the successes of other people. It's almost as if something is being taken from them when someone else receives special recognition or windfall gain or has remarkable success or achievement."

- Stephen Covey, *The 7 Habits of Highly Effective People*

Research has shown that abundance is a conscious choice and can promote happiness and lead to more positive outcomes. Scarcity mentality is fired by envy and is linked with poor wellbeing. We live in the age of envy. Career envy, kitchen envy, children envy, food envy, holiday envy. You name it, there's an envy for it.

"Envy is wanting to destroy what someone else has. Not just wanting it for yourself, but wanting other people not to have it."

- Dr Patricia Polledri, *Envy in Everyday Life*

In a recent large-scale longitudinal study on 18,000 people over a number of years, it was reported that envy is a powerful predictor of worse mental health. In addition, there was no evidence for the idea that envy acts as a useful motivator. Yet we live in a society that is systematically developing institutions, such as social media and new forms of advertising, that make people feel inadequate and envious of others.

> ### Give It a Try: Ways to Nurture *Mudita*/Abundance Mentality
>
> Take 5 minutes to think of all the good things you have done in your life.
>
> Stop comparing your life with others'. Be content with who you have become. For example, if you are going for a new job or a promotion, rather than comparing yourself with others, take an inventory of your years of experience, your contacts and network. If you have been laid off, instead of self-pity and envy, reframe the situation to see it as an opportunity to stop and reflect on what you really want to do with your life.
>
> Develop a tolerance for not getting what you want: Take note of all you have. See how much good is in your life – health, education, friends, life experience, time to enjoy what you have. Notice when you have envy at someone else's good fortune. When someone else has something that you want but don't have, recognise that you can survive without it, and that not having it does not make you less worthy or less of a person.
>
> Surround yourself with people who have an abundance mentality, that are happy for your happiness. If you are around scarcity-minded folks, who only show envy at your good fortune, this will dampen your enthusiasm for life.
>
> Spend some time noting exactly what a "good enough" life would look like.
>
> Incorporate gratitude into your life. See chapter 6. Include simple things that we might take for granted, like clean air. Keep a journal and write down everyone who has helped you in your life.
>
> Choose to approach life with an attitude of abundance instead of an attitude of scarcity.
>
> Actively practice *mudita* in your personal and professional life. Do not judge others in terms of what makes them happy. "Each to his own", as my mother would say. If your friend wants kids and you don't, be happy for them when their child is born. If you are a leader in your work, create an environment where you can positively influence your team, empowering and encouraging them so they can thrive. Praise them and give them credit. Celebrate their achievements. Avoid comparisons.

HOW MANY TIMES SHOULD WE FORGIVE? JUST ONE MORE TIME

"When I walked out of the gate, I knew that if I continued to hate these people I was still in prison."

-Nelson Mandela

I remember a client in her 40s whose anger and resentment for her father had preoccupied her for most of her life. When her mother died soon after her birth, her dad continued to raise her older brother and gave her to a close relative to be raised. He would see her a few times a year, for birthdays and Christmas. She felt betrayed and abandoned, though the family that raised her were kind and loving to her. The preoccupation and hostility we harbour serves only to hurt us. And she was very hurt.

As we spoke and imagined her father's situation in his mid 20s, perhaps perceiving himself unable to cope with raising a little girl, perhaps perceiving the girl would be better with more girls in a family and having a mother figure, perhaps fearing being judged by society in a negative sense in raising a girl on his own, perhaps.... all giving her dad the benefit of the doubt. And we all both need and deserve the benefit of the doubt. As we spoke her shoulders fell and her demeanour softened. Now and again, the old monologue would reappear and the anger would be refuelled.

Each time we remember an offence against us it triggers the old feelings of hurt, blame and rage. We need to reframe the story. We need to distract ourselves by saying STOP firmly to our monologue. And we need to keep doing it until we shift that groove which we have worn down the negative, angry, unforgiving ski slope to one of compassion and forgiveness. We do this not for the perpetrator, but for ourselves. My client needed to let go of anger not for her father, but for herself.

What do we mean by forgiveness? It does not mean that we try to decay the memory of the event. It does not mean excusing or denying the harm done. It does not mean reconciliation involving re-establishing a relationship with the transgressor.

So how do we know we have forgiven? When there is a shift in thinking; the desire to harm that person has decreased and the desire to do him or her good has increased.

Why forgive? Forgiving someone makes us less depressed, hostile, anxious, angry, and neurotic and more peaceful. It increases our self-esteem and leaves us more able to move on with our lives.

Give It a Try: Learn to Forgive

How to Forgive? Appreciate being forgiven. Imagine times in your life where, for example, you betrayed a lover and you were forgiven, and how it benefited the relationship.

Imagine forgiveness. When the client I just mentioned imagined her dad's situation, and imagined forgiving him, she did.

Write a letter of forgiveness. Consider the people throughout your life who injured and abused you, but whom you have never forgiven. Now detail the offence done to you. Note how you were affected and how you continue to be hurt. State what you wished that person had done instead. There is no need to send the letter; it is for your mind to ponder and your emotions to feel. For example, you might have a father who was alcoholic and you forgive him. Or you had a teacher who told you that you couldn't sing and you forgive her. Or a friend who used you.

Forgiveness takes effort and lots of practice. Start with "easy" forgiveness exercises before tackling more complex ones (like abuse). It takes practice and it produces empathy.

BRAINS SEEK PATTERNS WHERE NONE EXIST

"We are pattern seekers, believers in a coherent world, in which regularities appear not by accident but as a result of mechanical causality or of someone's intention."

- Daniel Kahneman, Psychologist and Economist

Do Bad Things Really Come in Threes?

Years ago, my partner and I experienced a bankruptcy while building our home. Two months later, my dad died suddenly. Within 3 months, our pet rabbit had to be put down. I remember feeling a relief that the three bad events were done and dusted.

Have you ever found yourself stepping over cracks in the sidewalk or knocking on wood? Or cherry-picking what you want from an astrology prediction? (this is linked to Confirmation Bias, mentioned earlier).

Scientists found the reason why bad things "come in threes" is really straightforward: they don't. We are a "Symbolic Species", the title of neuroscientist, Terrance Deacon's book on the subject. We can't help it. Our brains are pattern seekers. Deacon argues that the emergence of symbolic capacities unique to language was a key factor in the evolution of the human brain. As our prefrontal cortex increased in size so did our ability for symbolic representation; or perhaps it was symbolic reference itself that was the prime mover for the increased prefrontalization. Either way, we are pattern seekers.

But we go far beyond language in being a "Symbolic Species". We look for, create and find symbols everywhere – from the body language we use to the shoes we wear; from the car we drive to the choice of symbol that decorates our t-shirt. We use all to say something about ourselves that others in the "symbolic species" interpret intuitively according to the norms of that culture at that time.

Our brains' natural tendency to search for connections of seemingly unrelated subjects; from finding faces in different items like clouds, to having lucky numbers in a game of roulette; is called apophenia.

"Humans are pattern-seeking animals and we are adept at finding patterns whether they exist or not."
- Michael Shermer, *How We Believe*

Our brains are pattern-recognition machines that connect the dots and create meaning out of the patterns that we think we see in nature. Sometimes A is connected to B, sometimes it's not.

Sometimes this is true and helpful. It makes learning easier. For example, if you are given driving directions in an unfamiliar city, you can try to memorize each turn. But if you see a pattern -- for example, turn left, then right, then left, then right -- it will be easier to remember. It also helps process information regarding complicated situations based on past experiences. Master chess players use pattern recognition to develop strategies to play the infinite moves in the game.

Sometimes our tendency to recognize patterns is wrong and unhelpful. Look at gambling. People who are addicted to using slot-machines will argue that, since they have lost all their money so far, they are obviously "due" for a big win. This is demonstrably untrue — you always have the same, crappy odds at winning a slot machine no matter how many times you play. But the human brain looks at this pattern: "lose, lose, lose, lose, lose, lose, ___," and presumes that the blank *must* be a "win"! Many studies have shown that when people are tested with various situations of uncertainty, such as the stock market they will find patterns where they don't exist. It offers us a sense of self-control.

The problem is that sometimes it's hard to distinguish true from false patterns.

Beware of Pattern Seeking

Our brains have to quickly decide what information to focus on and what information to ignore, and can sometimes fall prey to negative biases that force us to focus on negative information.

Someone might make three mistakes and then do three things correctly; but if they ignore the three positive things, their brains will read the pattern as: *I never do anything right.*

Someone might take note of the three compliments they got today and another may look at the three complaints. At the end of the day, we see what we want to see; or, more accurately, we see what we are already biased towards seeing. Remember, biasing ourselves towards the positive is better for both our mental and physical health as well as making us easier to be around. Remember also that our brains are plastic and open to change.

Watch your thoughts for those negative patterns.

Our experience of the world is not objective. Our brains may be the world's best pattern-finders, but they are also the best pattern-inventors. The most important thing to realize about our neuroplastic brains is that they are forming patterns based on our subjective past experiences and beliefs but they do so through the lens of our current mind-set. Although you may not be able to change your past, you can certainly make efforts towards changing your present (and therefore your future) into a more positive one.

10.
DON'T BELIEVE YOUR THOUGHTS

"We are what we think. All that we are arises with our thoughts. With our thoughts we make the world."

— Buddha

Take a moment to consider how you think about yourself and the world in general. You will rehearse these thoughts thousands of times a day. Most of the monologue in our heads is a repeat of yesterday's. These thoughts become beliefs over a period of time, get etched into the fabric of our brains (literally) and engender a state of mind. So, becoming aware of our thoughts and being vigilant of which ones we choose to pay attention to will determine what way we interpret the world and ourselves.

Our thoughts lead to certain feelings and emotions, positive, negative or neutral. Watching our thought pattern and becoming gatekeepers for our thoughts, like overprotective loving parents to them, can help us to direct them along a negative or positive pathway. The choice is ours. Emotions trigger specific tendencies in our behaviour. For example, when we are angry, we tend to attack. When we are fearful, we tend to flee. Likewise, when we are positive, we tend to be more hopeful, more interested, more grateful, more serene, more inspired, more awe-inspired and to love more.

Positive psychologist, Barbara Fredrickson speaks about positive emotions "broadening" one's awareness and encouraging novel, varied, and exploratory thoughts and actions. Over time, this broadened behavioural repertoire "builds" coping skills and resources. Fredrickson's research has revealed that there are 10 positive emotions that are most commonly used to offset bad moods. The most frequent (and by far the most powerful) is love, followed by joy, gratitude, serenity, interest, hope, pride, amusement, inspiration and awe. Experiences of positive emotions broaden people's momentary thought-action repertoires, which in turn serves to build their enduring personal resources, ranging from physical and intellectual resources to social and psychological resources.

When our brains go into negative thought patterns, cortisol is released which narrows our thinking, our body is primed to escape and triggers the "fight or flight" response, and with it a cocktail of stress hormones. We will feel enhanced pain, our peripheral vision reduces, as does our ability to think laterally.

The physical benefits of acknowledging and disputing our negative thought patterns and replacing them with more compassion and acceptance help manage pain, headaches, anxiety disorders, heart disease, chronic fatigue, reduced immunity and gastrointestinal complications as well as make it more likely we will come up with novel and adaptive ways to reduce our problems.

Don't Believe Your Thoughts

I'm running late. Better see if I have any likes on Instagram. 0 likes...my life is meaningless. I've lost my keys. I must be losing it. I will never be recognized for what a great person I really am. People just don't know me. What am I actually doing with my life?

My kid got a note from the tutor. It is my fault. I am a terrible mother. I should really go for a run or do an aerobics class. Or maybe I will leave it until tomorrow. Would my neighbour's dog ever shut-up? I am sure she ignored me yesterday.

Does this sound anything like the monologue going on continuously in your head? We are on alert the whole time. We are constantly in a state of wanting, yearning or relief, expecting, obsessed with what happened in the past, or what's next, "toppling forward into the next moment". These heavy burdens of the past and projections of the future - we recognize them as "thoughts" - and most of our thoughts are tinted with a shade of dis-ease.

Most of us live with a low-level anxiety or a feeling of slight apprehension or worry which is flavoured with thoughts about our inability to cope now or in the future. This worry is sometimes free floating with no specific target, but it usually finds one. The thing is, this is normal. It is part of being human. We call it anxiety or worry. Buddhists call it *Dukkha* We think that we can calm this worrying mind by …travelling, moving to a bigger house, a cleaner house, getting a promotion, a pension, fame, the right partner, a child…and so on and so on.

But the feeling of unease is still there even when we get to the Canaries, even when our ten-bedroom mansion is spotless and even when the pension is in the post. It is our fundamental state and there is nothing wrong with it, except if we don't understand it or accept it for what it is. Why this might be our natural state is perhaps due to our living with constant uncertainty (whether we like it or not, this is true), lack of control (life is unpredictable) and a distant epigenetic memory from our ancestors' terrors living among the constant, life-threatening dangers of the savannah. We will always be a little anxious. But sometimes we get bogged down, or even depressed with negative thought loops. It is important to try and avoid negative thought trains.

First Things First –
Notice those Negative Thought Streams

Uneasiness, a persistent feeling of apprehension or dread or low-level worrying never helps, especially when we are in situations that are not threatening. It doesn't stop bad things happening. It just means you can't enjoy the present. So, what can we do to help our tired minds?

First, we have to become aware of our thoughts. Watch them like an objective observer. Acknowledge them for what they are.

A teaching from Tibetan Buddhism suggests that we relate to the thoughts that come up in our mind as if we were an elderly person in a playground watching children play. No matter what the thought might be, however fearful, remember that it's just a child, and treat it with a tender perspective, with compassion. And the thoughts will calm down, as with children.

We cannot think happy thoughts and worrying ones at the same time. In much the same way that David Wolfe, raw food guru, notes that we can either choose to put good food or bad food into our mouths, but not both. Most insidious worrying thoughts take us unaware, in the same way that we find ourselves mindlessly eating the chips or peanuts. When thoughts go unnoticed, it can complicate our response to life.

With awareness of what our thoughts are, and knowledge that we cannot have both positive and negative thoughts at the same time, we can use strategies like gratitude, savouring, being mindful for a moment, questioning the validity of our thoughts (see below) to stop the road train of negative thoughts before it goes into third gear, at which point it is much harder to control.

I am not referring to anxiety disorders here, such as panic disorders, or OCD, but just a general feeling of dis-ease that we all know and live with. But of course, sometimes these feelings persist and can almost become a personality trait. They can disrupt us from functioning fully and make us feel depressed. This is where we need to dispute them in the courtroom of our minds.

Bring on a Defence Lawyer
"It isn't events that disturb people, but their judgements about them."
- Epicetus

Almost anything in life can be seen from many angles. "Shit happens" - to all of us. A boulder falls on my car. I can be either upset and angry at this freak event, or I can enjoy the idea that the insurance will allow me to buy a car I prefer anyway. A fellow shouts at me from a passing car. I can either be aggressive back or I can try to imagine the hard day he has had and feel sorry for him. Stephen Covey introduced his "7 Habits of Highly Effective People" with a wonderful tale of being on a train and being angry at a man with free-range children who were disrupting everyone in sight. He was annoyed with the man's parenting skills. Then he found out the family were on their way from the hospital where their mother was dying. He softened his entire outlook on the family.

This brings us back to the notion that we generate our self-image like a lawyer (We are *not* Rational Logical Beings). We want a particular verdict and then we find the evidence to support it. We usually employ only one lawyer unfortunately: a prosecution lawyer – who speaks with the voice in our heads saying "I'm no good" "I'm a loser" "I'm unlovable" "he is a terrible father" and thereby jeopardizes our happiness and sanity. We need to keep a defence lawyer at hand, who tells us we are okay, lists our strengths, gives the other the benefit of the doubt, and provides evidence against those negative statements that the prosecution puts forward.

This court case never ends. But it helps to give as much support to the defence lawyer as we can, by continuing to supply her with accurate and up-to-date evidence, and in so doing rewire our brains to trend towards the more positive interpretation not only of ourselves, but others too. Once we realize that we can choose how to judge and interpret events, we have found the key to freedom.

Cognitive Behavioural Therapy 101
"Change your thoughts and you change your world."

- Norman Vincent Peale

Which brings us to the techniques of Cognitive Behavioural Therapy (CBT), an evidence-based talking therapy that can help us manage our thought patterns by changing the way we think and behave. It's most commonly used to treat anxiety and depression, but is also useful for other mental and physical health problems. It is also a great tool for managing the general worry and apprehension we all experience. CBT helps us to train our brains to have a healthier thinking pattern.

The basic idea is that "thoughts determine feelings." In other words, the monologue in my head is largely responsible for how I feel. However, this monologue of automatic thoughts is usually negative. They are automatic in so far as we don't really know where they come from. These thoughts lead to feelings which influence our actions and our actions influence our life.

These automatic thoughts are based on common problematic rules like:
- *"In order to be happy, I have to be successful in whatever I undertake."*
- *"If my spouse (sweetheart, parent, child) doesn't love me, I'm worthless."*
- *"To be happy, I must be accepted by all people at all times."*
- *"I have to complete everything on my "to do" list every day in order to be a success."*

So, the way CBT works is that we basically become aware of our automatic thoughts.

Mindfulness really facilitates this awareness process. Then we take a record of those thoughts, either on paper or mentally. This helps us to observe and understand our negative thinking pattern and where it comes from. We then bring a defence lawyer on board and dispute the thoughts with hard evidence to allow a more effective interpretation of the event.

Let me give you an example of how CBT works. A situation triggers a negative, automatic thought loop in our heads, often outside conscious awareness.
I said something stupid at the party and I am embarrassed and anxious about it.

I stop and become aware of the belief behind the thought.
I feel like a failure. I worry will they judge me. I'm always making stupid mistakes.

Now I consider the consequence, my emotional response and how I then behave.
If I continue to think so disapprovingly about myself, my negativity will affect my relationships and maybe my health. I'm exhausted.

And now the juicy bit…the courtroom in my head. Dispute, question and challenge distorted automatic thoughts. Irrational thoughts that influence our emotions are called Cognitive distortions in CBT.

Check what strengths I have overlooked. I try to be perfect. I am hard on myself. I don't have to be perfect. I'm not this critical of others who make the same mistakes.

Now nurture these effective new beliefs. Next time I react to something with an inappropriate level of sadness, anxiety or fear – I just stop and become aware. Rewind the tape of what just transpired in my head and ask myself: *What automatic thoughts led up to these feelings? What unspoken rules are they supporting?*

A couple of more examples you may be able to relate to. I am on a diet. I visit my friend, and have one slice of cake. And afterwards (maybe even during the tasting) I think to myself...*I am a loser; I blew my diet again* (Distorted Automatic Thought or Cognitive Distortion). Show me the evidence. One little slice is hardly blowing the diet. The truth of the matter is that *I only had one slice of cake* (dispute that automatic thought with some evidence). No need for punishment. *I enjoy the slice and then continue on the diet* (Effective new belief).

The project was delayed. *I screwed it up. I am a failure* (Distorted Automatic Thought or Cognitive Distortion). As a consequence, *I feel a failure and am now seeing other parts of my life that I mess up too. I feel under-confident.* I dispute, question and challenge these distorted automatic thoughts: *I've done well on other projects in the past. Maybe just this one is an exception. It's likely I will have success in the future* (Effective new beliefs).

Chorus of Negative Thoughts & Cognitive Distortions

We all have our own repertoire of automatic thoughts that seem to keep cropping up for us. Some of the more common ones are:

<u>Magnification and Minimization</u>: Exaggerating or minimizing the importance of events. One might believe their own achievements are unimportant, or that their mistakes are excessively important.
Magnify the negative: *I made a speech at a wedding and made a mistake. It was a terrible speech.*
Minimize the positive: *I have to pay so much tax. It's terrible (but I made so much money).*

<u>Catastrophizing</u>: Seeing only the worst possible outcomes of a situation. For example, worrying about getting a job. *If I don't get it, I will never get another job and will never have success in life.*

<u>All-or-Nothing Thinking</u>: Thinking in absolutes such as "always", "never", or "every".
I never do a good enough job on anything.

<u>Discounting the Positive</u>: Recognizing only the negative aspects of a situation while ignoring the positive. One might receive many compliments on an evaluation, but focus on the single piece of negative feedback.
I just got a job 'cos of luck.
I got only one like, my blog is stupid.

<u>"Should" Statements</u>: The belief that things should be a certain way.
I should always be friendly.
I must be thoroughly competent at all times, or else I'm incompetent.

Emotional Reasoning: The assumption that emotions reflect the way things really are.
I feel like a bad friend; therefore, I must be a bad friend.
I feel so angry at you; therefore, you deserve to be punished.

Jumping to Conclusions/Mind Reading/Fortune-Telling: Interpreting the meaning of a situation with little or no evidence.
I waved at my friend, but she didn't wave back. Maybe she is mad at me.
He yawned. He thinks I'm boring.
I'll go but I won't enjoy myself.
I'm not going to get that job.

Personalization: The belief that one is responsible for events outside of their own control.
My mom is always upset. She would be fine if I did more to help her.
My kid got a note from the tutor. It is my fault. I am a terrible mother.

Labelling: The tendency to make global statements about yourself or others based on situational specific behaviour.
I felt awkward during my job interview. I am such a dork.

Observing our negative thoughts, noting the cognitive distortion which we have applied to them and the resulting negative emotions, and then disputing the thought and underlying belief with evidence from other parts of our life has many benefits:
- Increases our self-awareness and self-understanding
- Recognises negative vicious circles
- Improves self-control, develops more functional cognitive and behavioural skills
- Reprograms our overlearned automatic thought patterns

Give It a Try: Which of these Cognitive distortions (irrational thoughts that can influence your emotions) **are you prone to?**

"Drag your thoughts away from your troubles... by the ears, by the heels, or any other way you can manage it."

- Mark Twain

Give It a Try: Cognitive Thought Record

Think of a situation which automatically triggered your thoughts or beliefs to be more negative and then made you feel bad

Then note the Cognitive Distortion in the Belief box that led to you feeling negative.

Dispute and challenge it and replace it with a more positive belief.

ACTIVATING EVENT	BELIEF	CONSEQUENCE	DISPUTE
SITUATION OR THOUGHT	NEGATIVE THINKING	HOW I FEEL	CHALLENGE THE THOUGHTS
eg. My wife didn't call when she said she would.	• She is angry with me (PERSONIZATION) • She is seeing someone else (JUMP TO CONCLUSIONS) • She doesn't love me (CATASTROPHIZING)	Anxious Jealous Angry Worried	• Maybe she got caught up at a meeting • Maybe she went shopping

COGNITIVE THOUGHT RECORD

What can you do if this situation arises again?

Knowing your tendencies, how can you prepare for the situation?

What can you do if you fall back on old habits?

Note when a negative thought occurs and write your Cognitive Thought Record once a day for a month and see how much better you will think and feel.

> **Give It a Try:**
> **What is blocking your happiness/your positivity?**
>
> Give some thought and time to the following:
> What I am doing that is disturbing my own inherent wellbeing and happiness?
> What is blocking my being positive about life?
> What is stopping me from being happy?

Overcoming Fears

"Fear doesn't exist anywhere except in the mind."

– Dale Carnegie

Whenever I put up obstacles to things that I feared doing in my life, my mother had a saying *"There is nothing stopping you but Canty's dog, and he is dead"*. Somehow, the blocking image of the dog and its disappearance would help clear the mental way for me to go ahead and try what I wanted or needed to do. The same idea has been repeated many times, perhaps more eloquently by others, to "feel the fear and do it anyway"!

> **Give It a Try: Dealing with Fear**
>
> Tune in to your most catastrophic thoughts and fears and examine how rational they are and how likely they are to actually happen.
>
> Identify the fears. Treat them as if they were being presented to you by someone whose goal in life is to make you miserable. Then argue back and rationally dispute them as you would to another person.
>
> Imagine the worst case scenario – what would be the very worst that can happen? You lose all your money. You lose your job. Your mother in law doesn't like you. You are unable to please everyone.
>
> Imagine the best case scenario – what would be the very best that can happen? You gain lots of money. You get the perfect job. Your mother in law does like you. You stop trying to please everyone.
>
> Imagine most REALISTIC scenarios.

"Fear is only as deep as the mind allows."

– Japanese Proverb

WHEN BAD MOODS, NEGATIVITY AND WORRY LURK

"When hatred with its package comes - you refuse delivery"
– Leonard Cohen.

When we become aware of them, our thoughts lose their power. For example, allowing ourselves to experience pain and negativity from an objective viewpoint and knowing that it will pass, is very useful and educational. Being aware that sometimes there is anger in us, and that our angry thoughts are searching out a target is also useful; especially if our awareness of the process can get there before the target is identified and we end up saying or doing something we will later regret. We realize that we can come to accept the negative thought, know that it won't cause us harm and in so doing, it loses its power.

> **Give It a Try: RAIN**
> **(Recognise, Accept, Investigate and Non-identification)**
>
> Stop now and again and consider your emotions, your feelings. Note what thought led to your feeling. And consider if there is a more realistic way to understand the situation. What evidence do you have to back up that thought?
>
> Recognize what emotions lead to what you feel in your body. Feel the emotion in your body...where are you experiencing it (heart? throat area?).
>
> Accept the emotion/feeling for what it is, just an emotion moving around you.
>
> Investigate it like you are a distant observer. And then know that IT IS NOT YOU. Distance it, watch it.
>
> Non-identification with the feeling will disempower it.
>
> For example, we can apply RAIN to when we are feeling anxious or angry. Recognize the discomfort in various parts of the body; without trying to change them or judge them, accept them and then further investigate them. Do they change over a short time; do they escalate? Finally, know that the emotions are passing through. Disempower them by not taking ownership of them. Rather than saying "I am angry", reframe it to "anger is passing through me and will pass".

Give It a Try:
HALT: Am I Hungry? Am I Angry? Am I Lonely? Am I Tired?

When we are feeling negative, we may need to HALT and check *Am I hungry? Am I angry? Am I lonely? Am I tired?* We might need to eat, or check out what caused the anger, or call a friend or rest. If we don't stop and consider, the cocktail of negative feelings can be misidentified and our reactions can cause more harm. We have all been there.

Likewise, for your relationships, if you know that your partner is experiencing one of the HALT emotions, best to help them to work through them before asking them for help or having a conversation.

Give It a Try: What is The Worst That Could Happen?

When my mother was feeling unwell with a chest pain, she asked my partner if he thought she would be alright. I remember eavesdropping on the conversation and was taken aback at his reply: "you either will or you won't, and either way, it will be fine". I was even more astonished at her response of peaceful acceptance and realization.

To care for our emotional landscape and when faced with worries, it often helps to imagine *what is the worst that can happen*? I once had a friend who lost many nights sleep when she thought her boyfriend's mother did not approve of her. When she decided to think of the worst that could happen…yes, the lady did not approve of her…she realized that that was not so bad and she could live with it.

It's when we try to change the emotions and fight them that they really get the upper hand.

Give It a Try:
Minimize Damage for Possible Stressful Moments

Some stressful situations can be anticipated and can be minimized or avoided completely with a bit of forethought and planning. For example: Always put keys, passport, glasses in one place,

Take photos of your passport, driving license, etc. and email it to yourself.

Make medical decisions in advance.

> **Give It a Try: Positivity Portfolio**
>
> Sometimes we may need tools to help us through times when it is hard to maintain a positive attitude.
>
> Keep a Positivity Portfolio – this could be a file of nice emails, positive comments, thank you letters, objects which remind you of good supportive relationships, or personal triumphs or anything that reminds you of your life at a positive, happy time.
>
> Refer to your portfolio when you are down – it may help to shift your mood back in line with your more positive self.

How We Reframe or Appraise a Situation Makes All the Difference

We often have a tendency to appraise a situation in a global, stable/unchanging, and personal manner, which is neither accurate nor good for our mental health. *I always break my diet; I never stick with anything. I didn't get the job and I'll never get one…*and on and on. We apply a global tendency to all parts of our personality and life, convince ourselves that it is our fault and take it personally.

We can equally apply the complete opposite interpretation: *the economy is not great at the moment* (not my fault), *I can try for another job* (it's not stable/unchanging) and *I got many jobs I went for in the past and no doubt will again in the future* (not global). The reframed interpretation is more likely to get us to send off more CVs and have more success.

Reframing our cognitive appraisal takes time and effort. Any time you catch yourself doing a negative, global, stable, personal appraisal, dispute yourself and find evidence to support that dispute.

Our Relationship to Our Experiences

The effect that experiences have on us, in both the inner and outer world, depends on our relationship to those experiences more than on the nature of the experiences themselves.

Take, for example, our relationship with our thoughts; let's say we are in bed worrying about the future. These worried thoughts lead to us feeling bad, but the fact is, nothing bad or threatening is actually happening now. The same goes for my relationship with others. If I am in a bad mood for some unrelated reason, I may have negative feelings toward someone I encounter. The next day, I may be in top form and feel that the people I meet (even the same unfortunate I met the day before) are wonderful!

Become aware of these relationships. Accept them for what they are. Don't let them drown you in a cocktail of stress hormones and negative thought loops.

The 'Musty' Side of Life and The Overthought Future

Musts fill our mental vocabulary. *I must shop. I must cook. I must go to the gym.* By reframing things, we can enjoy them so much more. *It is my pleasure and honour to shop for dinner and then to cook for my lovely family. It is my treat to myself to have an hour at the gym.* Unfortunately, if we think of these things as chores, they will generate feelings of resentment at worst. If we think of them as treats, we will feel better and energized to do them. Try to be less "musty".

We need to think of retraining our brains with memories just like we would fill our photo albums. We never see photos of divorces, only smiling weddings. In the same way, be a gatekeeper of what memories you want to ingrain into your mental pathways.

The other thing that we often fall prey to is overthinking something before the event.

I remember once while I was traveling in Mexico, a university in Perth contacted me about lecturing in a topic with which I was not familiar. The job was to start right away once I got back to Australia. I worried every night from the time I took the job until I actually started it. Will I be able for it? Will I be up to date with the current research? The rest of my holiday in Mexico was dampened and disrupted by my worrying. I got back to Perth; the job fell through.

Think of times when you worried about something and it never happened. Think of times when you worried and it never helped (and it never does). Keep reminding yourself of this in times when your mind is looking to the future and starts to worry. Pull the reins in and remind yourself that it will not help.

"I had a lot of worries in my life, most of which never happened"
- Mark Twain

What If My Negative Thoughts Are True?

"Supposing a tree fell down, Pooh, when we were underneath it?" "Supposing it didn't" said Pooh. After careful thought Piglet was comforted by this."

Maybe the tree did fall on top of poor Pooh and Piglet at a later date. Now, indeed some of these thoughts may be grounded on fact and are true. Indeed, people who are depressed are better than those who are not in recalling negative things that have happened to them. For example, they are more accurate in recalling both good and bad grades they got in school than those who are not depressed. Those who are not depressed tend to recall the good grades. But focusing on the negative, even if it is true, does not help us to function and be healthy.

DON'T LET STRESS OVERWHELM YOU

I'm late for a meeting. I can't pay the bills. Maybe she will divorce me. Will I be in time for the flight? What if the car breaks down? I need to move to a new home. I am getting married; all the expense and who to invite. I am not getting married…the list goes on.

We all know it. And how it feels. From minor challenges to major crises, stress is part of life. And while we can't always control our circumstances, we can control how we respond to them.

Stress is generally defined as conditions (psychological, physical or behavioural) that result when there is a discrepancy between perceived demands of a situation and perceived resources available to deal with it. So, I have an interview tomorrow, if I think I can cope, I look forward to it, if not, I stress. We can experience stress generated from our environment, our body, and our thoughts.

When stress becomes overwhelming, or it's chronic, it can take a toll on our well-being.

A stressful situation — whether it's something like being late for a meeting, or persistent worry about an ageing parent— can trigger a flood of stress hormones that produce well-orchestrated physiological changes. These stress hormones are the same ones that trigger our body's "fight or flight" response. Our heart races, our breath quickens, and our muscles get ready for action. This response was designed to protect our body in an emergency by preparing us to react quickly. But when the stress response keeps firing, day after day, it could put our health at serious risk. How many of us have had to get the report in on time, with high levels of stress, and kept going till the deadline (resistance stage) only to get sick when we finally finished and went on holidays (exhaustion).

It is important to remember that both a real-life event, (such as being late) or thinking about an event (imagining what will happen if we are late), have the same effect on the brain and produce the same ensuing stress response in our bodies. If left unmanaged, stress will reduce our immune function, contribute to many health problems, such as high blood pressure, obesity, diabetes, anxiety and depression and increase our vulnerability to various diseases, such as cancer, chronic pain and cardiovascular disease. It will have a negative impact on our quality of life.

It must be noted that mild stress, like just before an exam, facilitates an improvement in cognitive and physical function. However, if the intensity of stress passes beyond a predetermined threshold (which is different in each individual), it causes cognitive disorders, especially in memory and judgment.

How Can We Put the Brakes on Stress?

There is an Amazon forest of studies, reviews and meta-studies on breathing, meditation, yoga, etc. for managing stress. Whether you're about to be interviewed for a job or you're feeling overwhelmed by your divorce process, it's important to have some stress reduction tools that can lower your stress right now. Here are some short-term strategies that can be performed anywhere, take very little practice to master, are free and provide immediate relief. We will then look at some more long-term lifestyle changes that might help keep stress at bay.

"No matter what we eat, how much we exercise, how resilient our genes are, how skinny or young or wise we are—none of it will matter unless we're breathing correctly. That's what these researchers discovered. The missing pillar in health is breath. It all starts there."

- James Nestor, *Breath: The New Science of a Lost Art*

Give It a Try: Diaphragmatic or Belly Breathing

Lie on your back on a flat surface or in bed, with your knees bent and your head supported. You can use a pillow under your knees to support your legs. Place one hand on your upper chest and the other just below your rib cage. This will allow you to feel your diaphragm move as you breathe.

Breathe in slowly through your nose so that your abdomen expands, causing your hand to rise. The hand on your chest should remain as still as possible. Tighten your stomach muscles, so that your abdomen contracts, causing your hand to lower as you exhale through pursed lips.

At first, practice this exercise for a few minutes about three to four times per day. Gradually increase the amount of time you spend doing this exercise. Like anything else, practicing diaphragmatic breathing makes it easier. You may notice it takes an increased effort to use your diaphragm correctly. At first, you'll probably get tired while doing this exercise. But keep at it, because with continued practice diaphragmatic breathing will become automatic.

An alternative breathing exercise is as follows. Take a long inhale, and then exhale just a little and stop, a little more and stop and now exhale completely. Repeat this 3 times and then reverse it. Exhale completely and then take a sip of air, inhale just a little, and stop, then a little more and stop and now inhale completely. Repeat this 3 times. Return to normal breathing.

Give It a Try: Progressive Muscle Relaxation

Progressive Muscle Relaxation teaches you how to relax your muscles through a two-step process. First, you systematically tense particular muscle groups in your body, such as your neck and shoulders. Next, you release the tension and notice how your muscles feel when you relax them.

Step 1: Tension
Apply muscle tension to a specific part of the body. First, focus on the target muscle group, for example, your left hand. Next, take a slow, deep breath and squeeze the muscles as hard as you can for about 5 seconds. It is important to *really feel* the tension in the muscles, which may even cause a bit of discomfort or shaking. In this instance, you would be making a tight fist with your left hand. It is easy to accidentally tense other surrounding muscles (for example the shoulder or arm), so try to ONLY tense the muscles you are targeting. Isolating muscle groups gets easier with practice. Take care not to hurt yourself while tensing your muscles.

Step 2: Relaxing the tense muscles
Next step, quickly relax the tensed muscles. After about 5 seconds, let all the tightness flow out of the tensed muscles. Exhale as you do this step. You should feel the muscles become loose and limp, as the tension flows out. It is important to very deliberately

focus on and notice the difference between the tension and relaxation. This is the most important part of the whole exercise.

Remain in this relaxed state for about 15 seconds, then move on to the next muscle group. Repeat the tension-relaxation steps. After completing all of the muscle groups, take some time to enjoy the deep state of relaxation.

As you will be working with almost all the major muscle groups in your body, it is easier to start with your feet and systematically move up (or if you prefer, you can do it in the reverse order, from your forehead down to your feet).

It can be helpful to listen to someone guide you through these steps. Have a browse on the internet for a guided relaxation that suits you.

It can be helpful to say a certain word or phrase to yourself as you slowly exhale in step 2 (such as *"relax"*, *"let go"*, *"stay calm"*, *"peace"* *"it will pass"* etc.). This word or phrase will become associated with a relaxed state; eventually, saying this word alone can bring on a calm feeling. This can be handy during times when it would be hard to take the time to go through all the steps of progressive muscle relaxation.

Give It a Try: Autogenics

Find a quiet, comfortable place to relax. Ideally, this should be the same place you use each time you practice relaxation techniques. You can do these exercises lying down or sitting up. Make sure to remove your glasses and loosen any tight clothing.

Begin with your breathing. The first step is to slow down your breathing. Make sure you are in a comfortable position and start with slow, even breaths. Once you have slowed your breath down, tell yourself, *"I am completely calm."* Saying this to yourself may even be enough to put you in a state of relaxation.

Focus attention on different areas of your body. Start with your right arm and repeat the phrase, *"My right arm is heavy, I am completely calm,"* while breathing slowly and controlled. Do this again with your other arm and each of your legs, always going back to *"I am completely calm."*

Shift attention to your heartbeat. While breathing deeply, repeat to yourself six times, *"My heartbeat is calm and regular, slow and relaxed. My breathing is slow and relaxed, calm and comfortable"* and then say to yourself, *"I am completely calm."* This continues on for different areas of your body, including the abdomen, your chest, and forehead.

Give It a Try: Move, Exercise, Practice Yoga

Whatever suits you best, just try to move. Walk, run, cycle, practice yoga (yoga that includes mediation, breath work and physical postures have been found to be best for alleviating stress).

Do something– that suits your schedule, your finances, your energy and your lifestyle. If at first, you are put off. Try something else.

Give It a Try: Watch Your Thoughts

Our brains make plans for us, generate ideas, create, learn, and do so much more…and we need to be kind to them and give them a rest. Meditation is not stopping thoughts…they will keep coming (see chapter 3). We learn to look at the thoughts with a relaxed focused mind, a non-judgemental and kind mind. We begin to see the pattern of the storyline we keep telling ourselves and learn to take it more lightly. We watch for negativity, nervousness, discontent. We watch for thoughts that appear to justify or explain this unhappiness, but in reality, cause it.

PREVENTATIVE MEASURES AGAINST STRESS

"This too shall pass" - an adage ascribed to a range of sources from Persian fables and Buddhist monks to Abraham Lincoln. It echoes the temporary nature, or ephemerality, of the human condition - that neither the bad nor the good moments in life ever last indefinitely.

Our emotions are like the weather and the seasons. Storms come and go. Remember, as Rilke put it:

*"Let everything happen to you, beauty and terror
Just keep going. No feeling is final."*
Rainer Maria Rilke, Poet

Begin to develop an internal radar to monitor how your body feels and what emotion you are feeling. When your performance begins to slow down, do you automatically have another coffee? And when you feel stressed, do you turn to alcohol? What do you do when you feel tense? Where in your body is tense? Does your body need a rest? Or exercise? The following are some scientifically tried and tested ways to enhance your mood and help you to "broaden and build" your health and resources to weather blusters of life.

Expressive Writing

"Expressive writing gives us the opportunity to stand back and re-evaluate issues in our lives."
- Dr. James Pennebaker, Psychologist

Expressive writing has long been used as a tool in psychology to re-evaluate sources of grief and trauma. It can also be used as a method to enhance our positive emotions and help us to see clearly what we value. Writing helps construct a narrative to contextualize anxiety and organize ideas. Until we do this, the brain replays the same non-constructive thought patterns over and over and we become stuck. Put simply, we can dump what's troubling us out of our brains and onto the page. Writing helps achieve closure which tells the brain its work is done. This closure frees us to move forward.

It can be done anywhere, takes less time than a cup of coffee, it's free, and, best of all, scientifically proven to improve both how we process issues that compromise quality of life and things that can improve it.

Give It a Try: Keep A Diary or A Journal

Write for fifteen minutes a day for three consecutive days. Give yourself enough time to write uninterrupted. It is important to note that this is not a record for reading later. Its value is in the writing itself.

Identify a single issue you wish to address. Thoroughly explore the emotions and thoughts attached to this issue.

Ask yourself why you are experiencing particular emotions. Connect the dots. How does this event relate to relationships or events in your past?

Give It a Try: Write A Book of Quotes

Keep a record of wise quotes from various sources that you come across. I did this for years and would write them at the beginning of my yearly diary. When I needed a touch stone to lift me up or give me some perspective, I would look back at those quotes. I now know I was not alone in doing this.

Throughout history people from Marcus Aurelius, Michel de Montaigne and Tolstoy to Bruce Lee wrote such books to help navigate the challenges of being human and to help answer unaddressed questions. Why not join them and create your own book of comforting, inspirational and helpful quotes?

Write and Read Poetry

"Poetry interrupts the momentum of story, unweaves the narrative thread with which we cocoon our inner worlds."
- Maria Popova, *Brain Pickings*

Words matter. And the right words in a poem can elevate the intensity of our emotions. Rhythm and metaphor can tap into the less logical parts of our brain. Different research studies have found evidence that writing or reading poetry can be therapeutic for patients dealing with illness and adversity as well as their caregivers. Poetry therapy with a certified therapist has been found to help cancer patients improve emotional resilience, alleviate anxiety levels and improve their quality of life.

Give It a Try: Bring Creativity into Your Life

Don't forget that writing is not the only tool through which to express one's perception of life. Photography, sketching, painting, sculpture and many more avenues help us to see our world and ourselves. My brother makes short videos of what photos he has taken that day and matches it with music. A record of what stood out for him that day. A way to break the daily script, be creative and take note of the ordinary.

Music, Song, Dance
"Without music, life would be a mistake."
- Friedrich Nietzsche

If you have ever listened to music from when you were younger, you know how those songs can transport you and energize you. Music changes our mood. Music therapy is used to treat everything from depression, and anxiety to insomnia and pain. It is often used to help children and adolescents improve their communication skills and to regulate their emotions. Overall, it can increase our positive feelings. Engaging with music activates regions of our brains that influence everything from our memory, emotions, movement, to some involuntary functions. It releases endorphins and can help us relax.

Give It a Try: Bring Music into Your Life

Commit to listening to a piece of music for a set time. Make music. Sing. Listen to some music you love right now and dance. No-one is looking!

Be in Nature
"In forty years of medical practice, I have found only two types of non-pharmaceutical 'therapy' to be vitally important for patients…: music and gardens."
- Oliver Sacks, Neurologist

The healing power of nature has been recorded by poets, artists and psychologists. Nature eases our stress, improves our mental health and even increases our creativity. Environmental psychologists found that patients with tree views from their hospital beds recovered quicker, used less pain medication and were less anxious than patients with a view of a brick wall.

The ultimate gift of nature is the way it concentrates and consecrates time, grounding in a present both conscious of and undistracted by all past and all future.

After a paralytic stroke, Walt Whitman contemplated "what makes life worth living?" in his diary. His answer was *"Nature remains".*

Give It a Try: Be in Nature

Garden…if only pot plants. Have indoor plants. Have flowers in your home. Walk in nature. Watch nature programs. Go on a weekend camping trip and sleep beneath the stars.

Find People Who Are Calming

While Marie Kondo, The Queen of Clean is helping the world get rid of clutter, it is also important for our wellbeing and a maintenance strategy to clean out people from our lives who make us feel stressed.

> **Give It a Try: Be Conscious of Who You Spend Time With**
>
> Aim to surround yourself with people who have a calming presence, especially in times of extreme stress.

The Laughter Prescription

"Laughter serves as a blocking agent. Like a bullet - proof vest, it may help protect you against the ravages of negative emotions that can assault you in disease."

— Norman Cousins, Author

Laughter is therapeutic. In scientific research, the field of psychoneuroimmunology has found a tremendous positive impact of laughter on both our physiology and psychology.

It helps release endorphins, increases natural killer cell activity, increases levels of pain tolerance. It improves creativity, affect and helps relieve depression, anxiety, and stress.

Laughter has no side effects and is readily accessible.

> **Give It a Try: Laugh**
>
> Watch comedies.
> Re-watch your favourite sit-com. I do it with "Friends" when I need cheering up.
> Meet people who make you laugh.
> Go on social media and like as many pages as possible that make you laugh, so humour will show up more often in your feeds.
> Try not to take yourself seriously. Practice laughing at yourself.
> Do laughter yoga.

IT'S OKAY, EVERYTHING IS OUT OF CONTROL

An old Zen Story – "We'll see"

There lived an old farmer who had worked in his fields for many, many years. One day, his horse bolted away. His neighbours dropped in to commiserate with him. "What awful luck," they tut-tutted sympathetically, to which the farmer only replied, "We'll see."

Next morning, to everyone's surprise, the horse returned, bringing with it three other wild horses. "How amazing is that!" they exclaimed in excitement. The old man replied, "We'll see."

A day later, the farmer's son tried to mount one of the wild horses. He was thrown on the ground and broke his leg. Once more, the neighbours came by to express their sympathies for this stroke of bad luck. "We'll see," said the farmer politely.

The next day, the village had some visitors – military officers who had come with the purpose of drafting young men into the army. They passed over the farmer's son, thanks to his broken leg. The neighbours patted the farmer on his back – how lucky he was to not have his son join the army! "We'll see," was all that the farmer said!

Fact: Life is Uncertain

The Okinawan idiom *nankurunaisa*, roughly meaning "whatever comes is okay", has become famous because it functions as a powerful mantra. Basically, we never can know in advance how life will work out. If we don't mind what will happen next in our lives, we would have no reason to be worried today. Although this sounds like a ticket to emotional freedom and eternal happiness, most of us cannot help but care what happens next in our lives. It's what we have been taught since we were kids. Get a good education so we can get a good job, so we have enough money, and on it goes with making our lives as certain and secure as possible. We want to know what will happen next so we can rest in the moment knowing everything will be okay. But we can't control everything and sometimes our efforts to secure certainty leave us far from the life that we desire. And maybe keeping the notion of "we'll see" and *nankurunaisa* in mind would serve us better.

Our search for certainty affects how we face life, approach work and maintain relationships. We may choose a college degree with a particular career path in mind (often when we are 18 and clueless about both ourselves and life). At work we may lean towards a particular job with a "certain" future or pay grade. We may choose a partner that feels secure. We may engage in activities we know and with which we are comfortable. Sometimes these decisions work out great. But often, due to fear of the unknown, we ignore new opportunities, stifle creativity, ignore true desires, avoid risks and possible adventure for the sake of certainty. And let's not forget that nothing is certain, and even choices that seem sensible at the time can change when something unexpected happens. My mother would continually remind me in whatever situation I would find myself (both good and bad) "that could all change".

If we can find the courage to face the unknown and accept the chaos of life, we can "we'll see" our futures more gently. We can examine new ideas, go places we never expected to go, be more true to ourselves. We can be more content with whatever happens.

Mindfully releasing our need for certainty also creates more tolerance and patience as we give up our idea that the path we have chosen is the only way. Adopting a more accepting view of our path not only leads to less stress, and a greater sense of wonder, but maybe even happiness. It is amazing that the very thing we avoid can be the catalyst for creating the life that we really want.

"Do you want to know what my secret to happiness is? I don't mind what happens."

Jiddhu Krishnamurti, Philosopher

So how can we start to release our need for certainty?

Give It a Try:
Increase Awareness in Your Decision-Making Process

Are you choosing unhelpful or unfulfilling certainty over another unknown or uncertain potential? Review various choices you made throughout the day or week.

Ask yourself:
Did I make this decision for the sake of certainty?
Did I make this decision to feel more secure or to follow my heart?
Does this decision make me feel joyous or dreadful?
Do I think it will lead to new opportunities and experiences?
What if I wasn't afraid of the unknown, would I have made this decision?

If you find you are making more "certainty" choices than ones that align with your heart, rethink and reconsider. Face the unknown road ahead. Be expansive. And know that it is always a case of "We'll See" so it's all okay.

Give It a Try: Let Some "We'll See" into Your Life

The idea of "We'll See" reminds us that life unfolds more than one way. Just because we don't know the answer or we are unfamiliar with a problem, it doesn't mean that it won't work out. We'll see if what we are experiencing is good, We'll See if it will get better, We'll See if we can find a new way to handle the situation and still be okay. Just peek at some new possibilities and see how it feels. "We'll See" is an invitation to view life differently. The unknown often has unexpected gifts and benefits. "We'll See" can become the platform for making new choices more lightly because it shows us uncertainty is filled with dreams that have yet to manifest.

The next time something comes up at work, at home or in your friendships which causes you to experience a strong reaction, observe your feelings and thoughts. Notice if the mind begins to create futures based on what has happened, and perhaps you may even perceive how you react to those imaginary outcomes. Now try to apply the wisdom of "We'll See" – understand and accept that your projections are just that – projections. They have no reality in the now you are actually experiencing, and may well have no reality in the future you are imaging.

Give It a Try:
Think of Times You Took A Risk and How It Worked Out

With a mind-set of gratitude and positivity, start listing some risks that took you to places you could never imagine experiencing and people that you could never imagine meeting. Remembering how we have launched ourselves into the "We'll See" in the past can give us support and hope that life works out, and that somehow life supports us on the journey.

"All paths are the same: they lead nowhere. ... Does this path have a heart? If it does, the path is good; if it doesn't, it is of no use. Both paths lead nowhere; but one has a heart, the other doesn't."

- Carlos Castaneda, *The Teachings of Don Juan; A Yaqui Way of Knowledge*

NO MATTER HOW WE TRY, OUR MIND WILL ALWAYS FIND PROBLEMS

"But here I am in July, and why am I thinking about Christmas pudding? Probably because we always pine for what we do not have. The winter seems cosy and romantic in the hell of summer, but hot beaches and sunlight are what we yearn for all winter."

- Joanna Franklin Bell, *Take a Load Off, Mona Jamborski*

Have you ever found that when you are on your holidays, even though the weather is perfect, the beach is idyllic, the hotel is first class, you still find something to be a problem? Or when you moved into your perfect new home, the kitchen was your dream kitchen, the view from the bedroom was what you wished for, but then after a while you find the bathroom is a little cramped? And on and on. You get the idea. It's got to do with the way our brains work.

Harvard psychologist David Levari showed people hundreds of images of faces. They had to rate the faces as threatening or not-threatening. But there's a twist. As people saw more and more faces, Levari changed the ratio of scary-to-nice. He put in fewer and fewer threatening faces. Guess what happened?

People's brains moved the goalposts. As they saw fewer threatening faces, their standards for what constituted a threatening face went down. Now faces which had been seen as neutral before were deemed "threatening." And this effect was repeated in subsequent studies.

Fewer problems don't lead to more satisfaction; they lead us to lower our threshold for what is considered a problem.

"When a new comfort is introduced, we adapt to it and our old comforts become unacceptable. Today's comfort is tomorrow's discomfort. This leads to a new level of what's considered comfortable."

- Michael Easter, *The Comfort Crisis*

The quest to avoid discomfort and problems and just live in perpetual contentment will never end because your brain won't let it. It's an endless ladder where the finish line is always a little further away.

As mentioned in chapter 10, Buddhists call this *Dukkha*, and consider it a universal given of the human condition. And there is an old Arabic curse "May you get what you want when you want it".

"There are only two tragedies in life: one is not getting what one wants, and the other is getting it."

- Oscar Wilde

Our brain always finds problems due to its attempts to foresee and make an uncertain future a little more certain and safer. While this might seem logical, there's a fundamental flaw. It's the fact that our illusion of control is false. Of course, the really paradoxical thing is that we tend to think that if we worry more, things will turn out better. They don't!

11.
IF YOU WANT TO THRIVE WHILE ALIVE.... SLEEP

"Your performance at any moment during the day is primarily determined by what you did the night before—when you ate and how much you slept—because that is what sets your clock, which then primes your body and brain."

- Professor Satchin Panda, The Salk Institute,
*Circadian Code:
Lose Weight, Supercharge Your Energy, and Transform Your Health from Morning to Midnight*

400 years after Shakespeare so poetically called sleep "Nature's soft nurse" (Macbeth), the tone on sleep changed. Edison famously said "sleep is a criminal waste of time and a heritage from our cave days". He proudly slept 3 to 4 hours a night. Franklin noted "there will be sleeping enough in the grave". And in the 1980s UK Prime Minister Margaret Thatcher said "Sleep is for whimps." (She later suffered dementia). Neuroscience has now confirmed Shakespeare's medical metaphor, that sleep is very important to our health.

In an average life span of 80 years, we will spend 26 of them asleep. It is the single thing we will spend most of our life doing. Because it is so important. And this is linked to our circadian rhythm.

Our Circadian Rhythm – Light is The Key

A number of years ago I had the unique opportunity to live in a cabin in the woods without electricity for a whole year. It was in Ireland. That winter I slept on average for about 15 hours a night and in the summer (with long daylight hours) for about 5. Basically I, like a lot of other animals, slept with the natural light.

There is quite a variation in the average length that animals sleep. From koalas who spend up to 22 hours a day to elephants who only grab 3-4 hours of fragmented, disrupted and inconsistent sleep. This is linked to their circadian (Latin, meaning "about a day") rhythm.

In humans the average cycle is about 24.2 hours. The body's internal clock orchestrates rhythms of sleep, eating, body temperature, hormone levels and other processes.

Circadian rhythms make sure that virtually all the body's systems, from digestion and metabolism to temperature, blood sugar and cholesterol regulation, are optimized at various points during a 24-hour period. Circadian rhythms influence mental health as well, including the risk of psychiatric illnesses like depression and bipolar disorder as well as the potential for neurodegenerative diseases like dementia. These rhythms have an important influence on the immune system.

Different systems of the body follow circadian rhythms that are synchronized with a master clock in the brain. This master clock is directly influenced by environmental cues, especially light, which is why circadian rhythms are tied to the cycle of day and night. Almost every cell and every organ in your body has a clock synced up with this master clock. While other cues, like exercise, what we have just eaten, social activity, and temperature, can affect the master clock, light is the most powerful influence on circadian rhythms.

One of the most important and well-known circadian rhythms is the sleep-wake cycle. During the day, light exposure causes the master clock to send signals that generate alertness and help keep us awake and active. As night falls, the master clock initiates the production of melatonin, a hormone that helps with the timing of circadian rhythms and promotes sleep, and then keeps transmitting signals that help us stay asleep through the night. Melatonin is typically suppressed during the day and rises at night.

When properly aligned, a circadian rhythm can promote consistent and restorative sleep. But when this circadian rhythm is thrown off, it means that the body's systems don't function optimally. A disturbed sleep-wake circadian rhythm can give rise to various sleeping problems such as making it a struggle to fall asleep, waking up during the night or being unable to sleep as long as one needs. These can lead to fragmented and lower-quality sleep. Disturbed sleep-wake rhythm increases a person's risk of insomnia and excessive daytime sleepiness. This can have significant consequences on both mental and physical health.

Some of the culprits that disrupt our circadian rhythm are jet lag and shift work. There have been many studies suggesting health risks associated with shift work, including impaired cognitive performance, obesity, diabetes, depression, anxiety, reproductive disorders, decreased bone mineral density and shorter life span. In 2007 the WHO declared shift work a probable carcinogen. Accidents in the workplace have been found to be 60% higher in shift workers. Chernobyl and the space shuttle disasters both followed extended shift work and involved over-tired employees.

Indeed, any behaviour that puts sleep schedules out of whack with normal daylight exposure can cause a problem. There are no two ways about it: humans are diurnal. We're designed to be awake when it's light out and asleep when it's dark.

The problem is that these days all of us act like shift workers. We keep irregular schedules, and go to bed long after the sun has set. We often follow different bedtime schedules on weekdays and weekends. On top of that, most of us look at bright screens at night.

Importance of Sleep
While we may think our brains are at rest during sleep, think again! Sleeping improves our ability to learn, to concentrate, to process information, to make decisions, to consolidate memories and to fire creativity. Synapses are strengthened during sleep. A vital, complex, sophisticated cleaning process happens while we sleep which not only restores and refreshes our brains, but keeps Alzheimer's disease, among other dementia issues, at bay.

Sleep also helps restore bodily functions. Sleep allows us to have faster reflexes, better accuracy and reduces the risk of injury. It optimizes our metabolic fitness. It enhances immunity to infection, reduces the risk of diabetes, heart disease and cancer.

Suffering through one sleepless night after another can make us feel pretty rotten. But when we regularly lose sleep, we have a higher risk of physical illness and our mental health suffers, as do those around us! Staying up for 20 to 25 hours affects our performance more than if we were legally drunk (and it's not half as much fun!). Even simple activities, like having a conversation, become difficult. When we sleep consistently for 5 or less hours, we increase our chances of obesity by 50%. Anxiety, stress, and depression are some of the most common causes of chronic insomnia.

Having difficulty sleeping can also make anxiety, stress, and depression symptoms worse. It's a vicious circle!

Sleep is not an indulgence. It's not like going from economy class to business. If you don't sleep, you don't fly.

Do You Feel You Get Enough Sleep?

In the 1950s, people in the US slept an average of 8 hours a night. Now it is about 60 to 90 minutes less each night on average. That is a loss of 7 to 10 hours a week!

How you know if you are not getting enough sleep? If you need an alarm to wake you up, if you are irritable when you get up, and if you need caffeine to function.

How to Improve Sleep

Give It a Try: Seek Out Sun

Right after you wake up, go outside and get sunlight. Even if it is overcast. Exposure to natural light, especially early in the day, helps reinforce the strongest circadian cue. Get bright light in your eyes early to set your master clock. Your retinas are less sensitive in the morning and they will send strong messages which influence your "master clock".

Give It a Try: Get Daily Exercise, Practice Yoga

Activity during the day can support your internal clock and help make it easier to fall asleep at night. Avoid excessive exercise before sleep as it can spike cortisol and disturb your sleep.

Yoga has been shown to help insomnia in healthy adults. But note that it may take up to 12 weeks of regular yoga practice to see any positive effects for insomnia.

Give It a Try: Avoid Stimulants

Caffeine has an average half-life of 5 hours in a healthy adult. The half-life is the time it takes for your body to eliminate half of the drug. In other words, it will take until 2pm to lose half of the caffeine that is ingested at 9am. So, if you have a cup of coffee in the evening after dinner, half the caffeine will still be hanging around in your system for 4 to 5 hours.

Avoid stimulants like caffeine (coffee, tea, cola or any drink with caffeine) after lunch.

Give It a Try: Avoid Alcohol Before Bed

Alcohol stops us from getting into deep sleep. If we have alcohol the night before, we tend to wake up early the next day having had a disrupted sleep.

Give It a Try: Eat Light

Eating heavy food shortly before sleep disrupts our sleep pattern. Studies have found that people who get all their calories in an 8-11 hour window and stop eating 3 hours before bed are notably healthier.

Give It a Try: Limit Light Before Bed

Artificial light exposure at night can interfere with circadian rhythm. Experts advise dimming the lights and putting down smartphones and devices for at least one hour, or better still a few hours before sleep.

The brain mistakes blue light from smart phones, TV, iPad, etc. as sunlight. 10 minutes looking at a smartphone is the same for the brain as 1-hour walking in sunshine.

Brush your teeth in the dark.

Use the "Nightshift" feature on Apple devices (or the equivalent) to reduce blue light. Blue light isn't the only problem. ALL light is the problem. After dark, you want to reduce all light as much as possible. Optimally, you want as little light as possible after 8PM. As the day goes on, your retina actually becomes more sensitive to light. Since the cells in your eyes most relevant to timing and messaging the master clock in the brain are at the bottom of your retina, reduce overhead lighting as much as possible in the evening. Candlelight hardly triggers these cells at all. Light at night means less melatonin which means poor sleep which results in a foggy brain the next day. Keep the house dark at night.

Give It a Try: Follow a Consistent Sleep Routine

Varying our bedtime or morning wake-up time can hinder our body's ability to adjust to a stable circadian rhythm. Getting up late at weekends disrupts our rhythm. Studies show kids who sleep a consistent amount every night get better grades. Having a regular schedule for when you wake up, when you have your first and last meal, when you dim the lights, and when you go to sleep is a powerful combo.

Trouble Staying Asleep

It must be 4.30am. Maybe if I just turn over, I will be able to go to sleep. It seems like hours since I went to bed. Should I get up and check the time? I will be exhausted tomorrow for the presentation.

Sound familiar?

Give It a Try: Disturbed Sleep Hints

If you have a lot of problems with disturbed sleep, consider evening melatonin supplements (as well as all the other suggestions of course). Avoid sleeping pills. They actually lead to insomnia. Exercise sleep hygiene –

Reduce social media.

Listen to relaxing music.

Keep the room dark and slightly cool.

Set your alarm to go to bed, not to wake up!

Use your bed only for sleeping. Condition yourself to associate bed with sleeping only, not TV, video games, etc.

Muscle relaxation techniques, meditation and yoga help to induce sleep.

If you worry or have negative thoughts that keep you awake, play the alphabet game - think of vegetables, fruit or countries for each letter of the alphabet. Keep a journal by our bed and write negative thoughts down. It helps to get them off your mind and onto an external source.

Breathe. Do a body scan. Do a progressive muscle relaxation. (See chapter 10).

Waking up in the middle of the night, and sleeping in two chunks is natural. If you do wake up in the night, get up and do something for a little while (not on social media or the phone, maybe look at the stars) and then go back to bed.

What About Naps and Siestas?

Naps boost learning and alertness, even short ones of 5 minutes. 15 minutes can increase cognitive performance. 90 minutes can improve memory by up to 10%. Our performance on a learning task is best from about early morning till midday and then dips thereafter. How many of you have found that afternoon slump at work?

Naps rescue performance on all kinds of cognitive tests. Harvard psychologist, Dr. Sara Mednick found that heightened performance on a visual memory test was the same after a nap as after a full night's sleep. Performance dipped in controls who did not have an afternoon nap.

Creativity is boosted up to 40% after a nap. Many famous songs, (like "Yesterday" and "I can't get no satisfaction"), and books (like "Frankenstein"), were born after a nap.

Take More Breaks

We deteriorate in performance during the course of a day. We also deteriorate across a week. We use substances to make up this shortfall; 90% of Australians use caffeine to get through the day and the week. When we take more breaks during the day, and during the week, our performance actually increases. So, the take home message is: take more breaks, daily, weekly, yearly.

How Much Should I Sleep?

I have purposely avoided the question of how many hours of sleep we need. For years I read research which reported that sleeping too little or too much (which was usually less or more than 7 hours) was associated with a shorter lifespan. Trouble was, a lot of the subjects in those studies who slept for longer periods had co-morbidities like depression, so of course, the results were skewed. We also need to ask subjects in sleep studies questions like; what is your daily routine? are you a manual worker? a heavy exerciser? etc.

We often don't notice sleep debt. 8 hours may not be enough for you. Maybe with 10 hours you might perform even better. It seems 10 hours of sleep is better than 8 for creativity and information processing.

When I attended a 9-day silent retreat with Ajahn Brahm, a London-born, highly esteemed Buddhist monk based in Perth, Australia, I expected a gruelling schedule of wake-up calls at 4 am. I had done many Vipassana silent retreats before, with bells to call us to mediation. But Ajahn Brahm forbade bells. In fact, he encouraged us to listen to our bodies and to sleep as much as we needed and wanted. He was right in reckoning that all us city folk, working 9 to 5 and constantly checking our phones, were sleep-deprived. The first few days, I slept for probably 10 to 12 hours a day. Others told me later that they too, having been given both a venue and the encouragement to sleep for the first time in their lives since before school, slept way more than usual. And we all felt more refreshed as a result.

My answer to how long you should sleep follows the advice of John James Audubon, the great American ornithologist, "When the bird and the book disagree, believe the bird." Don't listen to what you read in Cosmopolitan or online, listen to your body. See how you feel when you wake up ...and note the 3 questions: did you awake without the alarm? were you refreshed and alert? and did you function perfectly well without caffeine? If you answer yes to all of these, then you slept enough.

THE FABRICATED PAST AND THE IMAGINARY FUTURE

"The world you see is just a movie in your mind."

- Jack Kerouac

My sister is only a year and a bit older than me. When we recount memories from our childhood, her stories are often so different to my memory of the same events that it is hard to believe we were in same situations. How many times have you experienced an event with a friend, say a party, and you come away with completely different stories of what happened?

Perceptions are collages, not photos. Collages constructed from our knowledge, beliefs and memories. Every psychology 101 class is entertained with a wide range of perceptual illusions to bring this point home to us. From the Muller Lyer illusion (where most of us see the lower line as longer than the one on top) to the parallel line illusion.

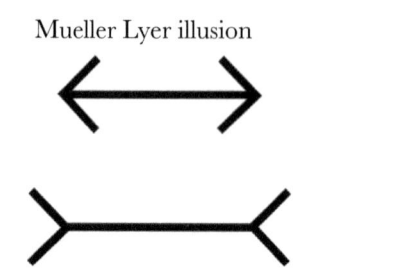

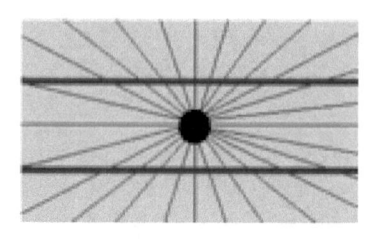

Mueller Lyer illusion

Beyond visual illusions, our entire experience of our world is created by our perception, using all kinds of psychological shortcuts (such as the fundamental attribution error and confirmation bias mentioned earlier) preconceived beliefs and conditioned expectations. We reconstruct our memories and form our imaginary future in the same creative manner.

The Past and Future Are Illusions

We tend to make our story of who we are by how and what we remember of our past and how we imagine our future.

Let's first look at our memory of the past.

"Memory is suggestive, subjective and malleable"
— Elizabeth Loftus, Psychologist

Remembering the past is fundamental to being human. Our personal memories give us a sense of continuity – the same "me" traveling through time. Personal memories are essential for social interactions. Being able to recall personal memories provides important material when making new friends, forming relationships and maintaining ones we already have. Memory helps us to solve problems and to regulate our emotions. As already noted in chapter 10 it helps when we are feeling sad to take time to dwell on a positive memory.

But memory is notoriously unreliable, especially when it comes to details. Have you ever recalled something from your childhood (or indeed from more recent times) only to find out that it actually happened to your sister and not in fact, you? How many times have you misremembered events that may have never happened or which occurred at a different place and time? Indeed, if you are anything like me, how many times have you started to look at a movie, or started a book, only to realize half way through (at best) that you had seen or read it before.

Scientists have long known the "suggestive, subjective and malleable" nature of memory. For example, they have found that prompting an eyewitness to remember more about a crime they have witnessed can lead them to generate details that are outright false. These 'memories' are, in fact, wholly invented, but they feel just as real to the witness as actual memories.

Elizabeth Loftus and colleagues at the University of Washington asked a group of people to watch videos of traffic accidents. After watching the film participants were asked to describe what had happened as if they were eyewitnesses. They were then asked specific questions, including the question

"About how fast were the cars going when they smashed each other?"

One group of participants were given this question and the other four groups were given either the verb *'collided'*, *'bumped'*, *'hit'* or *'contacted'* in place of the word *'smashed'*. The participants estimated the car speeds differently depending on the words used. The word *smashed* provoked the highest estimate. Next highest was *'collided'*, then *'bumped'*, and the slowest was the verb *'hit'*.

The "eyewitness" participants in this experiment were also asked either *"Did the white car jump the red light?"* or *"Did a white car jump the red light?"* These two questions elicited very different responses in the eyewitnesses. Those who answered the first question all said either yes or no. While the second group questioned as to whether there was a white car or not in the video. There was no white car in fact.

In our daily life, this tendency isn't a flaw, it's a feature. We can't possibly remember every tiny detail we see, but our memories would feel incomplete if there were big gaps through them. So, the brain fills in the details as best it can, borrowing from other memories, suggestions and imagination in order to build what feels like a complete picture.

Everything we remember is remoulded in the present. Take a moment to read the list below and then cover it.

- Bed
- Rest
- Awake
- Tired
- Dream
- Wake
- Snooze
- Blanket

- Doze
- Slumber
- Snore
- Nap
- Peace
- Yawn
- Drowsy

Which of these were NOT on the list: Bed, doze, sleep, gasoline? The last one is easy to spot, but most of us are fooled by "sleep". We got the gist and our mind filled in the gap. And we had already been prompted!!!

Memory is a compost heap in a constant state of reorganization and reconstruction.

Each time we recount our past we are merely reconstructing the story from the last time we spoke of or recalled the event. The original is long since a foam bubble, forever gone, only to be reconstructed not from some objective indelible record of the past but rather in line with how we perceive the world as we see it NOW. We don't retrieve memories, we fabricate them. We fill in details (often very different to the original) that were not stored.

We have many different kinds of memory, such as episodic memory (for events or episodes), autobiographical memory (the story of me), procedural memory (a type of implicit memory which aids the performance of particular types of tasks without conscious awareness; such as tying shoe laces, or riding a bike), etc. The episodic and autobiographical memories are prone to artistic licence!

"A key rule about memory change over time is what we call fade-to-gist."

- Dr. Charles Brainerd, Psychologist, Cornell University

We lose the details of an experience rapidly but retain our understanding of its gist much longer. After visiting India, we may quickly forget what we ate and where we stayed, but remember that we had a great experience and the feeling we have is good. Or indeed, we may only remember the tummy aches, and the late trains and have an overall bad feeling.

According to the American Bar Association, of the 21 wrongful convictions overturned by the Innocence Project in 2011, 19 involved eyewitness testimony. More than three-quarters of wrongful convictions that are later overturned by DNA evidence are based on eyewitness reports. The legal system finally acknowledged this problem, when the New Jersey Supreme Court instructed judges to tell jurors that "human memory is not foolproof" when considering eyewitness testimony in a case.

The shortcoming of memory, or rather the necessity to reconstruct memory, is that we compare two subjective experiences NOT occurring at the same time – now, as we recall the event and then, when it happened.

Think about the following:
- What were your political views when you were 25? You will possibly give your current ones.
- How much alcohol did you drink when you were a teenager? You will probably underestimate or overestimate, depending on how things are now.

A flashbulb memory is a vivid, long-lasting memory affected by our emotions when we first learn of a very surprising or emotionally arousing event, for example, hearing the news that President John Kennedy had been shot. Much research has done on such events. Researchers interviewed more than 3,000 individuals from seven US cities about their memories of learning of the terrorist attacks of September 11, 2001 as well as details about the attack, one week, 11 months, 2 years and 10 years after the attack. 20% of the details remembered just after the event were lost a year later. Despite the significant editing of the memories over the first year, interviewees' confidence in the accuracy of their recall remained high over the 10 year period.

The strong emotional reactions elicited by flashbulb events were remembered more poorly than non-emotional features such as where and from whom one learned of the attack.

Perhaps most interesting was the finding that the levels of media attention and ensuing conversation were correlated with accuracy of episodic memories. The more media coverage there was of the event, the less consistent was individuals' memory of the event. This suggests these two variables should figure critically in any account of retention of episodic memories. Both media coverage and repeated recounting of the event increase the degree to which the memory of the event is degraded. How many of us think we remember our first day at school? Our parents have told the story over and over again to family and anyone willing to listen, and somehow, we believe that it is we ourselves are recalling the event.

A great deal of what we consider to be our life story is inaccurate. One personal example from my own life. When I was in my 20s in the 1980s, I cared for an old lady in Palo Alto. We would watch Judge Judy together daily. Or so I told myself and others over the years. But Judge Judy didn't actually start airing until 1996! I had told the story many times until one day my niece pointed out that it could not have been so. I conflated my memory of the events to myself and others and made it a reality. This is just one simple example of how our memory is fabricated.

"Everything we hear is an opinion, not a fact. Everything we see is a perspective, not the truth."
– Marcus Aurelius

We could add our memory of the past to this list of unreliables.

How do You Imagine Your Future?
"The future depends on what you do today."
- Mahatma Gandhi

165

No matter how hard you try, no matter how badly you want to, there is no way to truly know the future, and the world isn't *really* organizing itself to give you hints.

We spend 12% of our day thinking and creating expectations about our future, what Dan Gilbert, a social psychologist at Harvard University so beautifully called "nexting" in his book "Stumbling on Happiness". We are constantly toppling forward into the next moment. Watch yourself during the day and note how often you think - either looking forward to it or worrying - about your future.

Our ability to think about the future has a big impact on how we think about happiness. According to Gilbert, the ability to imagine is the brain's greatest achievement. "Nexting" gives us a sense of control. We have a hard time imagining that we will be very different in the future than how we see ourselves today. It is hard for us to believe we'll feel and think differently in the future; that we will want different things, have different opinions on things.

As we saw in chapter 1, when we observe people in dire conditions who report being happy, we are inclined to think, "Nonsense! How can they be happy? They must not know what happiness feels like." Not only are we poor in imagining what is going on in the minds of others, it's hard for us to even to imagine our future selves.

A few common flaws when it comes to thinking about our future;

- We tend to mis-imagine our future (another bit of good news…so don't worry about it).

- We tend to think the future will be much like the present. For example, many folks regret getting tattoos, especially if they got them when they were in their early twenties. The common reasons being that their personality changed or the tattoo doesn't fit their present lifestyle. They got someone's name that they're no longer with. The tattoo is no longer meaningful.

- We tend to want to exercise control over our future.

- We tend to hold on to our beliefs even when evidence proves those beliefs to be wrong. This is called Belief Perseverance. People expend considerable mental energy to maintain their beliefs when presented with facts that prove them wrong. An experimenter asked subjects to look a series of pairs of photos of people and choose which is most attractive to them and why. Then in a sleight of hand, the experiment switched some of the choices. Not only did the subjects not notice that the photo of the one they found less attractive was now presented as their first choice, they were able to justify why they preferred them. We tend to stick to our initial belief even when evidence contradicts it. Such as that red wine is good for our hearts…it's not.

- We tend to underestimate the novelty of the future. There has been a litany of faulty forecasts by scientists who always err on predicting a future that is too like the present. For example:

    - *X-rays are bunk* - Lord Kelvin, 1900
    - *There is not the slightest indication that nuclear energy will ever be obtainable. It would mean that the atom would have to be shattered at will* - Albert Einstein, 1932
    - *I think there is a world market for maybe five computers* - Thomas Watson, Chairman of IBM, 1943

When we imagine the future, we are responding to what's happening now. The imagination doesn't take into account that we end up feeling differently once the imagined future occurs. Imagination adds and subtracts details, and we don't see that the features we populate our idea of the future with are either made up or will be missing altogether once the reality emerges.

The Future We Imagine is Almost Always Too Smooth

Have you ever happily and willingly made plans to babysit your nieces or nephews several weeks in advance, only to find that you became more and more reluctant to the whole idea as the day drew nearer? Have you ever agreed to go to a party a week in advance, only to want to sit and watch Netflix when the time comes? After we eat Christmas dinner, we vow never to eat again. But when we said yes to babysitting and the party it was because we felt good about the prospect then.

When we think of future, we think of WHY (general) and NOT HOW (details). Many mothers regret giving up their career to raise their child, but at the time they were thinking about the broad concept of being a mother, not the gritty details of what is involved.

"When we remember or imagine a temporally distant event, our brains seem to overlook the fact that details vanish with temporal distance, and they conclude instead that the distant events actually are as smooth and vague as we are imagining and remembering them."

- Dan Gilbert, *Stumbling on Happiness*

That's because when we imagine the immediate future, i.e., tomorrow, we think in much greater detail. But if you imagine a random day next year, it will be varied, vague and comfortable. In short, it will be free of all the actual details, discomforts and the reality of the day itself. I am moving to a new country; it will be wonderful with no hiccups!

The great irony is that people actually believe that their projections about these smooth future events are just as accurate as tomorrow, with all of its known details.

Psychological Immune Systems Act As A Buffer When Traumatic Events Happen: "Hey, That Wasn't So Bad After All!"

Our psychological immune system keeps our illusions and our realities in check. It's a lot like the body's immune system, which protects us from illness. If our immunity is too low, we fall ill. If it's hyperactive, the body's immune system starts to attack the body. And our psychological immune system is very similar. A healthy psychological immune system helps us feel good enough so we can cope with life, but just uncomfortable enough that we're driven to improve our situation.

A friend of mine lost her leg when she was around 20 in a train accident in India. She went on to become a renowned dancer in a dance company for people with disabilities. She said it was one of the best things that ever happened to her. Our psychological immune system transforms the meaning of terrible events when they happen to us. A more common event that many of you may be able to relate to is getting a job. *I didn't get the job I applied for and really wanted at the time, but you know, it all worked out for the best, cos I got this job which I now love.* The fact is it's easier than we think both to rationalize loss, and to overcome it. This means that we can stop worrying about bad things that might happen to us because even if they do occur, our psychological immune system is there to serve as a buffer and soften the blow.

So, in summary, our brains use TODAY in our conceptualizations of both yesterday and tomorrow. Our past memories and future imaginations are actually pretty similar to the present moment. We don't really know as much about our own experience of the past or the future as we assume we do.

It's very difficult to extract ourselves from what we now know and believe, to sneak back into our former self and speak objectively about how we felt then - without being influenced by the experiences we gathered between then and now. And the same applies to our future selves. We can try to imagine how happy we'll be if this or that thing happens. But the truth is, by the time that thing happens, how much will we have changed?

12.
LIVE YOUR OWN STORY

"If we wish to know about a man, we ask 'what is his story--his real, inmost story?'--for each of us is a biography, a story. Each of us is a singular narrative, which is constructed, continually, unconsciously, by, through and in us--through our perceptions, our feelings, our thoughts, our actions; and, not least, our discourse, our spoken narrations. Biologically, physiologically, we are not so different from each other; historically, as narratives--we are each of us unique."

- Oliver Sacks, *The Man Who Mistook His Wife for a Hat*

Who Am I Anyway? Your Reality Distortion Field

In February 1981, Bud Tribble, one of the key software developers on the original Macintosh computer, borrowed a term from Star Trek, (where it was used to describe how the aliens created their own new world through mental force). He noted that "Steve Jobs has *a reality distortion field*." Basically, Jobs, Apple's co-founder, had "unrealistic optimism", an ability to convince himself and others that anything is possible.

We all have our own reality distortion field. It defines who we are, our abilities, our limitations, our strengths and our weaknesses. This is the reality we project to the world about ourselves. That *perceived* reality becomes our *actual* reality. We believe it. Others believe it. It's our story. If you think you are no good with people, you will never practice your people skills at a party. If you see yourself as the life and soul of the party, you will be just that. If a teacher told you that you were no good at languages or math or gym you likely still believe them and have lived the role since then.

The thing is, our views of ourselves (and others, and indeed life in general) determine what we perceive to be true, which in turn forms our thoughts. Over time these thoughts get etched into that ski slope of our brains and they become our beliefs.

How we arrange the plot points of our life into a story can shape who we are - and is a fundamental part of being human. The way we choose to tell the stories of our lives, to others and - crucially - to ourselves, becomes an integral part of who we are. As we repeat the story, it becomes more ingrained. Our beliefs become our reality. The plot seems real. Very often our story is influenced by our parents, our peers and our culture and we act our way through life according to what is considered a "normal" blueprint such as "go to school, graduate, get a job, get married, have kids."

"Life stories do not simply reflect personality. They are personality, or more accurately, they are important parts of personality, along with other parts, like dispositional traits, goals, and values."

- Dan McAdams Nietzsche, Professor of Psychology, Northwestern University

As we remember and continuously rehearse the facts, events, and beliefs, we weave them into a story - our story, our personality, our identity. Pretty much from birth, we are "actors." We have roles to play—daughter, sister, etc. As we interact with the world, we make decisions and choices, and become the "author," so to speak, of the play of our lives, when we begin to bundle ideas about the future with experiences from the past and present to form a narrative self.

When I first learnt the fragile and unreliable nature of my memory, on the one hand, I felt it undermined my life story. Had I been telling myself and others lies all these years? On the other hand, it gave me a tremendous sense of freedom. Some of the stories I had been telling myself about myself, others and events over the years were untrue and I could just bin them forever. They were no more than fabrications.

What is extraordinary and simple and exciting about our "reality distortion field" is that it can be changed. In the same way as we choose what to read, what to wear, who to spend time with, we can choose what way to think about ourselves and things in general. Our stories can be changed. Narrative psychologists have long used this knowledge to help people live better lives.

If we want to be more positive and less critical, then we need to practice that. Again and again, day after day, thought by thought. We literally reprogram and rewire our brains by repeating our stories.

Know Your Script, Your Story

"The self is constructed out of narratives... we don't spin our tales, they spin us! There is no self at the core...Rather it emerges as "the center of a narrative gravity"

– Daniel Dennett, Philosopher

I worked with deaf people in Ireland and Australia. And although I was researching sign language and cognition, the thing that struck me the most was their sense of identity, the story they told of who they were. And there was a lot of division, both in terms of whether they used sign language and if they had a cochlear implant. Were they 'deaf' or were they 'Deaf'? The latter meant they were in the Deaf community and that was their story. Many of their hearing parents either joined in the Deaf community fully or left. It seemed there was no middle ground. We hold tight to our stories, our political beliefs, our religious and cultural traditions, all of which form our personality and our identity.

Give It a Try: How I Tell My Story

Take a few minutes to write your story, a brief description of yourself and your life. Write from the third person perspective, perhaps as if you were a close friend or work colleague. If you need some ideas for personality traits, have a look at the constructs in the grid below. Note important events in the past and possible future and why they are meaningful.

Like detail	Big picture thinker
More down to earth	Artistic
Anxious	Relaxed
Pessimistic	Optimistic
Disorganised	Organised
Conscientious	Less reliable
Agreeable	More hard-headed
Shy	Outgoing
Neurotic	Relaxed

Who Exactly Are You?

"Who we are is a story of our self — a constructed narrative that our brain creates."

- Bruce Hood, Cognitive Neuroscientist,
The Self Illusion: How the Social Brain Creates Identity

We are shaped by the era, the expectations, the media, the people, the songs, the ideas, etc. that we have been fed since we were born. Bob Dylan puts it succinctly when he sings "I Contain Multitudes", the multiplicity of selves in him.

We all behave differently with different people, at different times of the day and when we are in different moods. For example, doctors have been found to make more accurate and faster diagnoses when they are induced to be in a positive mood rather than in a negative or neutral mood. But they don't realize it. Women are much more likely to have an affair when ovulating than at any other time of the month. This behaviour is entirely subconscious.

This begs the question; how do we know how we are supposed to behave or indeed how we will behave? Do we really have that much control over it? Seems not!

Among other things, our cultural environment has a huge influence on us. Our cultures and what they expect of us influence us in the way we perceive ourselves. For example, depending on where we were brought up, we tend to either overestimate or underestimate our own qualities or abilities in relation to the same qualities and abilities of other people.

We, particularly in Western cultures, discount unflattering or troubling information that contradicts our self-image in order to preserve a favourable identity and positive self-regard. We do this unwittingly. We don't even know we are doing it. In this way we avoid being confronted by contradictory information that can make us uncomfortable and uneasy. Like a lawyer we can find evidence to keep our pre-existing conclusions about ourselves safe and sound. We often select our own strengths and the other's weaknesses when making peer comparisons, in order that we appear better on the whole. For example, many doctors tend to overestimate their ability in communication with patients. In other words, they have made conclusions without evidence. They are like lawyers!

In America most people overestimate their IQ. Sometimes called The Lake Wobegon Effect, after a radio program about a fictional town, the closing words of which were always "Well, that's the news from Lake Wobegon, where all the women are strong, all the men are good-looking, and all the children are above average." At the other end of the scale, East Asians tend to underestimate their own IQ and abilities in comparison to others, in order to improve themselves and get along with others.

Few things limit us more profoundly than our own beliefs about what we deserve, and few things liberate us more effectively than daring to broaden our horizons of possibility and self-permission for happiness. The stories we tell ourselves about what we are worthy or unworthy of - from the small luxuries such as naps to the great luxuries such as a creative calling - are the stories that shape our lives.

Bruce Lee knew this when he warned that *"you will never get any more out of life than you expect"*.

Give It a Try: Become More Aware of Your Story

Survey 5 of your friends to see a trend in how they perceive you.

Reflect less, notice more: Your calendar and your credit card bill will tell you more about who you really are than that story you're spinning in your head.

Ask "what" not "why": "What" gives you answers you can use. What you want says a lot about who you are.

Consider and then write down your values.

Note inner dialogue; Be mindful.

Take Control - Write Your Own Script

"People construct stories about their lives, much as a biographer would. We weave what we can observe (our conscious thoughts, feelings, and memories, our own behavior, the reactions of other people to us) into a story that, with luck, captures at least a part what we cannot observe (our nonconscious personality traits, goals, and feelings)"

- Timothy Wilson, Professor of Psychology,
Strangers to Ourselves

If we want to change behaviour, we need to change our story.

When we believe that something will affect us in a particular way, it often does. If you want to be extraverted, act like that. If you want to be less fearful, then "do it anyway". If you want to be prosocial, then do volunteer work.

If you are attached to a particular identity (too bossy, complain too much) and don't like it, then change it as you would a jacket, by changing your behaviour. Live your new story and your brain will, with repetition, believe it. My mother put it another way – *"think big, act big and you will end up big"*.

Every Thought We Think Is Creating Our Story - Affirmations

Although we may not even be aware of it, every day we mentally plant seeds in our brains with thoughts of love or hate, acceptance or rejection, success or failure. Affirmations broaden our perspectives and help us to see things in new ways. When we train our brain to "ski down the slope" of positive affirmations, it is surprising what it can do for us. Positive affirmations can help block negative thought tracks from repeating themselves. Athletes now routinely use affirmations – *You can, you can, you can.*

"Self-affirmations can be viewed as mental seeds that grow a new self-narrative about your self-worth, values, and competence."

- Donald Altman, Psychotherapist and former Buddhist Monk

For many years since my 20s, I have written both affirmations and inspiring quotes in my dairies for each year. Yes, there was a time when we had paper diaries! I would glance at them before a lecture to give me confidence or at times when I knew I was going down. They really helped. And I always had them nearby.

Have a read of these self-affirming mantras. You may find these or similar affirmations of help in times of difficulty.

- I am open and accepting.
- I am good enough.
- I forgive myself.
- I trust the process of life.
- I am willing to let go.

- I am at peace.
- I welcome miracles into my life.
- It's only a thought, and a thought can be changed.
- The point of power is always in the present moment.
- Every thought I think is creating my future.
- Don't take anything personally.
- My day begins and ends with gratitude.
- The past is over.

Give It a Try: Write 3 Affirmations about Yourself

1.
2.
3.

Give It a Try: Rewrite Your Script

"Please yourself, and you please everyone" was one of my mother's mantras. She encouraged me to ignore what others' thought I should be or do. Sometimes we behave in ways that we believe pleases others, and not ourselves necessarily. Indeed, some of us may live a life, do a job, even marry a particular person to please someone else. I have had friends who had children just to please their parents; friends who took up particular careers just to please their parents.

If there are parts of your life that you are living just to please others' version of your script, consider how much it is costing you emotionally. Take some time to reconsider changing course to be more aligned with what resonates more naturally with you.

If there is something that you might like to change in your behaviour in everyday situations, use the information you wrote above about how you see yourself as a starting point for writing a short description of what that change might look like. Maybe think of things you admire in others (creativity, curiosity, open mindedness, bravery, persistence, vitality, loyalty, kindness, citizenship, leadership, forgiveness, humility, prudence, gratitude, hope, humour).

Spend around 2 weeks role playing out those new behaviours. Focus on changing behaviour rather than the way you think. To help with this process ask a friend to role play some situations with you. Rather than thinking that this is permanent, think that your old behaviour is on holiday and you simply have an opportunity to act like a different person.

If you are unhappy with your current story, note what is not working for you and stop reinforcing it. Ask yourself: what do I want my life story to look like at the end of the day? Remember, *"Please yourself, and you please everyone"*.

Our Stories Are Not Coherent Storylines with A Crescendo at The End

"We become the autobiographical narratives by which we "tell about" our lives"

– Jerome Bruner, Psychologist

An acquaintance of mine who really doesn't know me very well asked me a few years ago what I was going to do next with my life. He insisted that I always had a plan, especially as he recounted what he knew of my life thus far …get the Ph.D., lecture in various universities around the world, move to the countryside. He somehow forgot that few lives are a linear, rational story. Most of us live without much sense of a direction in our narrative. Many of us change our careers, partners, country, whatever, many times in our lives. We tend to pare down our story to critical moments when we are recounting who we are. And after the fact, we follow a kind of narrative structure, as if it is a coherent, intentional, evolving story line building up to a fulfilling climax of where we are now. Remember not all storylines build to a crescendo! Life is open-ended, unpredictable and like a house, never finished.

> **Give It a Try:**
> **Write a Letter to Yourself as If It Is In 10 Years' Time.**
>
> What would you tell a younger you?
>
> Is there anything you keep telling yourself and others about your story that no longer serves you?

LIFE IS A SERIES OF "NOWS" THAT ENDS IN DEATH

1988　　　2020　　　2088

There is no security, no certainty. We really do not have control over what will happen to us. We tend to make our story of who we are by how and what we remember of our past and how we imagine our future. But our memory is like a soap bubble with no substance, and our projections for the future are usually clouded with worry. There is no solid "I" that needs to be improved. Our "self-illusion" is constantly changing. Aspiring to live with pure awareness, recognizing the ball and chain of our memory and our warped relationship with time is our best bet.

"You cannot compare this present experience with a past experience. You can only compare it with a memory of the past, which is a part of the present experience…

To understand this is to realize that life is entirely momentary, that there is neither permanence nor security, and that there is no "I" which can be protected.

To understand music, you must listen to it. But so long as you are thinking, "I am listening to this music," you are not listening."

- Alan Watts, *The Wisdom of Insecurity*

Living with awareness, realising that our memory and projections for the future are unfounded, and acknowledging our warped relationship with time can help us live with the fact that that there is neither permanence nor security, that there is no "I" which can be protected and that death is the only inevitable.

And in the end…. life is a short holiday – contemplating our death might help us make the most of it.

"Unfortunately, the clock is ticking, the hours are going by. The past increases, the future recedes. Possibilities decreasing, regrets mounting."

- Haruki Murakami, Japanese Author

"Stop whatever you're doing for a moment and ask yourself: Am I afraid of death because I won't be able to do this anymore?"

- Marcus Aurelius

Life is limited. We are all going to die.

Death is often characterized as something negative or evil. We imagine the grim reaper as someone waiting around the corner, prepared to torment us at any time. When someone passes away, we talk about how they were taken far too soon. However, it is unfair to characterize death in this way. Rather than being good or evil, it is simply natural. It happens to each of us and is a stage of our life that we have to accept, just as we embrace the transition from youth to old age.

Death is often spoken of in euphemisms. When did he pass away? When did you lose your husband? Deceased, departed, kicked the bucket, etc. Many of us spend our lives running from death, searching for medicines that will prolong both our youth and life. Considering that what comes after death is unknown, this is an entirely valid response.

It makes intuitive sense to ignore or avoid the topic of death. Nobody wants to go on vacation constantly thinking about the fact that the trip is going to end soon. That's no way to spend your week in Spain. But if psychology teaches us anything it's that our brains don't always work the way we think they do.

Researchers at the University of Kentucky and Florida State University had people think about death and the result was... they got happier. They showed more concern for those around them and tended to be more grateful for the life they now experienced, recognizing 'what might not be'.

"The scientists concluded, 'Death is a psychologically threatening fact, but when people contemplate it, apparently the automatic system begins to search for happy thoughts.'"

- Michael Easter, *The Comfort Crisis: Embrace Discomfort to Reclaim Your Wild, Happy, Healthy Self*

Thinking about the fact that the holiday will end makes us better appreciate the beach because we don't delude ourselves into thinking it's forever. We savour it and don't take it for granted. Importantly, we make better choices about what to do with our days, our weeks, years and life. It helps us focus on what's important.

Time is limited, so we must make the most of it. When we keep death on our minds, we can focus on what truly matters and helps us build mental boundaries and so avoid letting time pass through our fingers.

"Let us prepare our minds as if we'd come to the very end of life. Let us postpone nothing. Let us balance life's books each day. The one who puts the finishing touches on their life each day is never short of time."

- Seneca

In the current average human lifespan, we get around 4,000 weeks to live. How to meaningfully approach our human transience and how to use this relatively short holiday on earth is challenging and exciting. Of course, much of that time will be spent on mundane activities such as *"Six weeks waiting for a green light. Three months doing laundry"* (David Eagleman in his book "Sum: Forty tales from the afterlife" see chapter 7). In 2020, COVID was a wake-up call for a lot of people about death and the limited nature of life. And also about their priorities. We don't want our life to be like that awful moment on Sunday evening when the work week looms and we say, *"Where did the time go? I didn't do all those things I wanted to do."* The discomfort that comes with thinking about death can spur us to live better. To make the most of it.

Because some day it will be our last day and we will die.

Artists, poets, philosophers and indeed all of us at some point ponder on the interplay between the beauty and terror of being alive as we drift daily toward the infinite. When the American artist Keith Haring became aware of his impending death in his early 30s, he wrote how its proximity charged living with life:

"I think I finally realize the importance of being alive. Life is so fragile. I think it is very important to be in love with life. I have met people who are in their 70s and 80s who love life so much that, behind their aged bodies, the numbers disappear."

Let Death Be Your Advisor

"Let each thing you would do, say, or intend, be like that of a dying person."

- Marcus Aurelius

Life is full of stresses and problems, great and small. Sometimes these can overwhelm us, or at the very least can hijack our good intentions and abduct us to a place where we are grumpier, meaner or nastier than we ever meant to be. At these times, contemplating the inevitability of our own death, and that of everyone we hold dear, can help us shift gears and take stock of what really matters. A brief moment of understanding, and of deep appreciation for the moment we find ourselves in, however difficult it may appear to be, can emerge. This is using our impending death wisely, as an advisor and counsellor.

Give It a Try: 6-Word Memoirs of a Life

Ernest Hemingway was once challenged in a bar bet to write a novel in just six words and he came up with "For sale: baby shoes, never worn." It started a trend in "Six-Word Memoirs". Here are some examples

"Cursed with cancer, blessed with friends."
"I still make coffee for two."
"Should never have bought that ring."
"Tombstone won't say did not try."
"Finally realizing: I AM good enough."

Write a 6-word memoir or biography of your life. Or a haiku. Or draw your life.

"Death is the only wise advisor that we have."

- Carlos Castaneda, *Journey to Ixtlan*

Give It a Try: Write Your Own Obituary

Here are some examples of obituaries of famous people;

Spike Milligan's Tombstone – *I told you I was sick!*

Mother Teresa - *Spread love everywhere you go. Let no one ever come to you without leaving happier.*

Write your obituary. How would you want to be remembered?

REWRITING OUR STORIES OF OTHERS
– EVERYONE IS DOING THEIR BEST

We Never Know What Is Going on in Others' Minds

"An Anthropologist on Mars" is the title neurologist Oliver Sacks gave to his book about encounters with folks with neurological disorders. The title was drawn from his meeting with Temple Grandin, a woman with autism who is a world-renowned designer of humane livestock facilities and a professor at Colorado State University. The title of this book comes from a phrase Grandin uses to describe how she often feels in social interactions. In her own words, she's an "anthropologist from Mars".

Typically, autism can be characterised by profound difficulties with communication and imaginative activity. It can also include bizarre behaviours such as repetitive rocking, an indifference to ordinary social cues and an inability to understand what others are thinking or feeling. Some people with autism have difficulty being aware of the mental and emotional states that they, or those they are interacting with, are experiencing. This ability is commonly called a Theory of Mind in psychology.

Theory of Mind is one of the foundational elements for social interaction and is important as it provides the ability to predict and interpret the behaviour of others. It is the understanding that others have beliefs, desires, intentions, and perspectives that are different to our own. Psychologists have long known that deficits in Theory of Mind can occur in people with autism spectrum disorder, schizophrenia, cocaine addiction and other conditions. But all of us, autistic or not, often find it hard to understand what is going on in the minds of others.

I once worked with the parents of a deaf child. Born deaf, he had gone to a deaf school and learnt sign language. When he was about 13 or 14, it was discovered that a cochlear implant could significantly improve his chances of hearing. His parents went ahead with the operation and indeed, he recovered his ability to hear. He was furious. He complained of the constant noise and chaos. He missed his silence. He missed his identity and his Deaf world. Most hearing people would probably think that a deaf person would want to hear given the chance.

Lori and George Schappel are conjoined twins, share their blood supply and even their skull. They are very different people. Lori is outgoing, likes to drink and is a successful bowler and George is a country singer and a member of the Church of Jesus Christ of Latter-day Saints. But there are certain things the sisters undeniably share. And though they have two distinct brains, they are of one mind in their opinion about whether they would ever consider undertaking the risks of surgical separation. They said that while they live separate lives, they would never want to be surgically separated. Any able-bodied person would think that a conjoined twin would want to be in a separate body. The attitudes of the Schappell sisters are strongly felt, but not unique. Indeed, in her book, "One of Us: Conjoined Twins and the Future of Normal," Alice Dreger, a historian of anatomy at Michigan State University argues that the assumption among surgeons, the public and most parents, that life as a conjoined twin is not worth living, and that separation should be tried in nearly every case, whatever the risks, is an outsider's premise, and one in need of some serious scrutiny.

The bottom line: we don't know what is going on in others' minds.

Give it a Try: Listen

Listen to others' opinions and beliefs with an open mind and with no judgement. The best way to understand others is to listen to them.

Everyone Is Doing Their Best

"Every Saint has a past.
Every Sinner, has a future."

- Oscar Wilde

When a sneaky negative thought appears, perhaps about the noisy neighbour or the boring colleague, we need to be vigilant and immediately think of all the fine qualities he or she has and the many times they helped us out.

After giving a talk at a hospital about how to apply these aspects of practical psychology, one lady wrote me an email:

My husband never clears up his dishes after dinner and I used to go on in my mind with a list of complaints of the dirty slob. But after I consciously thought that we are all doing our best, I began to remind myself quickly before the train of negativity about him got into third gear, that he takes out the rubbish, fixes anything that is broken in the house and reads to the kids (although he still is a slob). My feelings towards him have softened.

If there is one thing I used to emphasize again and again to my counselling students, it was that everyone is doing their best, given their upbringing and circumstances. Our main duty is to remind them that they are wonderful human beings, because they have either forgotten or no one ever told them and they need to know…and we will hopefully help them with behaviour issues.

**Give It a Try:
How to Rewrite Your Story of Someone That Causes You Negativity**

Having difficulty with an in-law? Or a colleague?

Sometimes, if we need something more tangible than a switch in our thought processing it helps to actually take a piece of paper and write all the positives about the person that is aggravating you or causing you anger on one side and the negatives on the other.

Then fold the paper in the middle, tear it in half and throw away the negatives side. Reread the positives.

Note the positives of your partner, child, etc. Maybe even tell them what you appreciate about them, or what they did and continue to do well.

WE ARE NOT AS UNIQUE OR AS CONSISTENT AS WE THINK

"We are more alike, my friends, than we are unalike."

- Maya Angelou, Author

Have a quick read of the following and assess how accurate is this description of your personality?

You have a need for other people to like and admire you, and yet you tend to be critical of yourself. While you have some personality weaknesses you are generally able to compensate for them. You have considerable unused capacity that you have not turned to your advantage. Disciplined and self-controlled on the outside, you tend to be worrisome and insecure on the inside. At times you have serious doubts as to whether you have made the right decision or done the right thing. You prefer a certain amount of change and variety and become dissatisfied when hemmed in by restrictions and limitations. You also pride yourself as an independent thinker; and do not accept others' statements without satisfactory proof. But you have found it unwise to be too frank in revealing yourself to others. At times you are extraverted, affable, and sociable, while at other times you are introverted, wary, and reserved. Some of your aspirations tend to be rather unrealistic. Security is one of your major goals in life.

If you kept nodding to yourself thinking "Yup, that is so me", then you have just fallen victim to what has come to be called the Barnum or Forer Effect. In 1948 psychologist Bertram R. Forer gave a personality test to his students. Promised a unique personality assessment they had to rate it for accuracy on a scale from 0 to 5. The average score was 4.26.

But everyone received that exact same text you read above.

I gave the same test to a group of my university psychology students and they were impressed with how accurate their personality assessment was. When I revealed the Forer Effect in that each got the same assessment, one student stood up with an air of revelation saying "we are all the same!".

The trick is that all the statements are so vague they could apply to literally everyone. But as long as you believe they are about you in particular, you fill the gaps with your own meaning. So it appears to be a super-tailored personality assessment. Further studies of the effect have shown it works on everyone, regardless of their belief in the supernatural or their cultural background. It is the strongest when:

- you believe the analysis applies only to you
- you believe in the authority of the evaluator
- the analysis lists mainly positive traits

This is why horoscopes in your daily newspaper say exactly the same things but with different words. Why many fortune tellers know you like you know yourself. *"You will have a big challenge this week. At first it will be difficult, but you will find the strength you need to overcome. Focus on relationships."*

Of course, we can compare ourselves negatively to others as well. In an era when we are constantly bombarded with images on social media, images of others showing them happy, beautiful and successful, enjoying exotic locations and delicious meals, it's easy to feel that our own lives are dull, ordinary and mundane in comparison. Now known as "The Instagram Effect", this can lead us to a very distorted view of how we compare ourselves to our peers. Of course, nobody tends to post a photo which makes them look bad. On the contrary, many photos posted on social media have been retouched or altered, so we are comparing ourselves not, in fact, to our peers but rather to a fantasy version of them. Our own reality has a hard time matching up.

The take-home message is not so much not to trust personality tests or horoscopes, nor to quit all your social media accounts, but rather to realize that:

- We are more alike than we are different
- We are always checking each other out and erroneously thinking we're the only ones doing so
- Our comparisons of ourselves with others are founded on partial information and probably have very little value

Coming back to the Fundamental Attribution Error, which makes us ascribe poor personality for faults and failings in others, but circumstances as being the cause of our own failings, it is important to remember one thing: We are all doing our best.

A Broader View

"Since everything is but an illusion,
Perfect in being what it is...
One might as well burst out laughing!"

- Longchen Rabjam

We are all conditioned by the culture we were dropped into and by those around us. Gender roles are learned. As are the sense of time, space, language, group pressure, cultural stereotyping, religious beliefs, etc. With this realization, we can be more spacious and can be more accepting and forgiving of ourselves and others. As we essentially create our story as we go along, within the perimeters of our conditioning, we synthesize our own happiness or its opposite.

Being more objective and seeing the world from a broader point of view can help our relationships, both with ourselves and others, immeasurably. A great deal of our suffering and anxiety stems from our tendency to mistake our experience of the world for understanding reality. By replacing the confusion of our own narrow simplified interpretation of how things appear with a broader awareness of reality, we can begin to be more objective - and in this way be more understanding and forgiving.

Wisdom traditions have questioned the nature of identity for millennia. Our most up-to-date neuroscience also points to the 'self' as an entity less well defined than the one we instinctively believe in. It may be of great benefit to be open to questioning the narrative, the script and the identity which we have clung to as our "self".

"YOU ARE GOOD ENOUGH" – SELF-IMPROVEMENT IS AN OXYMORON

"I can only think seriously of trying to live up to an ideal, to improve myself, if I am split in two pieces. There must be a good "I" who is going to improve the bad "me." "I," who has the best intentions, will go to work on wayward "me," and the tussle between the two will very much stress the difference between them. Consequently "I" will feel more separate than ever, and so merely increase the lonely and cut-off feelings which make "me" behave so badly."

- Alan Watts, Philosopher, Writer

A couple of years ago I read pretty much all the "self-help" pop psychology books I could get my hands on. Everything from Covey's "7 Habits of Highly Effective People", Dale Carnegie's "How to Win Friends and Influence People", Victor Frankl's "Search for Meaning" to Brené Brown's "Daring Greatly", Tony Robbins' "Giant Within", Eckhart Tolle's "Power of Now and "A Whole New World Now" and a whole heap of others. I wanted to get an overview of what people were reading in the field. And I came to the conclusion that there were generally two camps of thought: self-improvement and self- acceptance (and indeed this includes general acceptance of life and of others). The former seems to suit the business model while the latter is more in line with the long-haul of coping with life. Personal experience, the Stoics, the Buddhist traditions and indeed science tend to support the latter approach in general.

I take especial issue with the very notion of self-improvement — something particularly prominent in the season of New Year's resolutions, major goal setting, and an attempt to control life. Essentially, it reprimands the self at the very root.

Happiness and more especially contentment are not a matter of improving ourselves or others, or our experience, or even merely confronting those things, but of remaining present with life in the fullest possible sense. Pain is best dealt with by accepting it. Dealing with others is best achieved by accepting them as they are. Life's ups and downs are borne more easily with acceptance.

"You are good enough" is a mantra that parents need to tell children, we need to tell others and we all need to tell ourselves. Over and beyond accepting ourselves just as we are, we sometimes deny ourselves the privilege of ignoring our social conditioning and daring to be ourselves.

Your Signature Strengths

I remember as a young kid, my teacher, a nun, told my mother that I was good at drawing, but we only drew in class for about an hour a week and maybe bringing me to after-school art classes might be a good thing to do. My mom did. I loved it. Because the school I attended did not generally encourage art, I found it hard to give it value, but I loved it and still do. Hence the cartoons in this book!

In his book "Authentic Happiness", Martin Seligman outlines 24 personality traits, such as justice, courage, temperance, creativity, honesty, humility, love of learning, teamwork, spirituality, etc. which we all have to a lesser or greater degree. He calls those which are strongest in each of us "signature strengths".

Seligman tested a large group of people on various positive psychology strategies and found that one of the most effective strategies to increase happiness was the following: participants were asked to take an inventory of character strengths online at www.authentichappiness.org and to receive individualized feedback about their top five "signature strengths".

They were then asked to use one of these top strengths in a new and different way every day for one week. They found that when participants were asked to identify and use their signature strengths in a new and different way every day for one week, they were happier and less depressed afterwards and this effect lasted for 6 months.

Give It a Try: Using Signature Strengths in A New Way

Hop on www.authentichappiness.org and do the Values in Action Signature Strengths questionnaire VIA. It takes a few minutes and it is a useful glimpse into what your strengths are.

Once you have done this, give yourself a challenge to do something which exercises your personal strengths every day for one week.

Dare to be Fully Yourself

"To be yourself in a world that's constantly trying to make you into something else is the greatest achievement".
                                                                          - Ralph Waldo Emerson

My mother constantly reminded me "Please yourself and you please everyone". It is easy to let other people (no matter how well-intentioned), society and the conditioned voices in our heads tell us what to do and what not to do. To know what's important to us, what we love and what brings us joy, and to pursue it, against the odds, takes courage and intention. We don't want to come to the end of our lives and realise we never dared to be ourselves and that we had been living the wrong life. The only person who can tell you who you are and what song you were born to sing, is you.

I love music and always wanted to be able to play a musical instrument but remembered how I was told in school how I was no good at it. About 5 years ago when I was giving seminars on which this book is based, I thought I should take my own advice. I started taking piano lessons. Already in my 50s, with no music experience at all, I thought it would be neat to be able to play a few tunes, expand my neuronal pathways to keep my brain healthy and stop listening to myself say how I would love to play a musical instrument. It wasn't easy to get my head round reading the music, or translating it into getting my fingers to move where they were supposed to. But with time, I began to entertain myself.

> **Give It a Try: Dare to be Fully Yourself**
>
> Do one thing this week for you that you have been putting off because you are too busy with family, work, etc. Whatever you always wanted to do, do even a bit of it this very week. It doesn't have to be earth shattering. Just find something you have always wanted to do and start.
>
> Be a photographer. Take photos with intention. Be a painter, paint. Be a dancer. Dance. It doesn't have to be ground-breaking. Just do a little of what you may have been putting off for years – just for you. Challenge yourself to do something that resonates with you and commit to it.
>
> It's a cliché but - just do it. Nobody is watching and nobody cares, but you.

The myth that happiness can be found somewhere, sometime - but not here or now - persists and proliferates. Tic-toc and Instagram gurus promise a better, happier life if only you will follow this program, do this workshop, take this supplement. The tragedy of this endless pursuit of happiness is that it leads us to, quite literally, miss the point - we can sacrifice contentment for an illusory future happiness.

On the other hand, a great many real and lasting benefits for ourselves, others and society can be achieved by committing to implementing strategies which lead to changes in the way we see the world, deal with ourselves and others - perhaps implementing some or all of the "keys to contentment" in this book.

If we are trying to choose between the self-help and self-acceptance schools, perhaps we need to apply a little of both in order to achieve a balance between pursuing a happier, better life and allowing ourselves to realize that deep, meaningful contentment may already be within our grasp - right here and right now - if we can just allow ourselves to stop, notice and enjoy it.

"Contentment is the highest happiness"
- The Buddha

AFTERWORD

"Life is like a box of chocolates; you never know what you are going to get"
-Forrest Gump

I recently read Yuval Noah Harari's "Sapiens, A Brief History of Humankind". 4 things I learned from this breath-taking ride through our entire human history from our evolutionary roots to the age of capitalism are: first, there is an element of luck in everything that happens to us; second, things are not always getting better; third, change is integral to life and fourth, all our beliefs are conditioned by the era and society into which we are born. These are issues that we need to accept both at a macro level, in the history of mankind, and at a micro level in terms of our own lives.

So, when we pride ourselves or beat ourselves up (or indeed others) for success or failure, we must remember that elements beyond our control are responsible. Our lives, though we may be led to believe the contrary by the media and societal expectations, will take their own pathways - pathways which may not necessarily always be leading us to a better place. Whatever that might mean to us. The beliefs I hold, from women's rights and equality to environmental sustainability and democracy, are ideals that I have been conditioned with by the society and period into which I was born, and are not in fact indelible truths. And finally, change is inevitable in all our lives, no matter how much money, or insurance or assets we might accrue, and death is, as Colleen Hoover wrote "the only thing inevitable in life."

In spite of all this and indeed with an insight into all of this, I believe that if we try to understand and accept how our minds work, we can, with some strategies integrated into our daily life, be content with the uncertainty of life, accept the discontent which is inherent in our human nature and the inevitable death that awaits each of us. In other words, to be content with where we are at and the way things are. I hope that implementing some of the strategies in this book, which have been verified by science or born from deep wisdom and experience, will help you live a happier, healthier and more contented life.

And remember to eat the chocolates and savour them along the way!

"Our life is a quest for gratification. There is physical gratification in health, in satisfying the lusts of the body, in wealth, sexual love, fame, honour, power. All these gratifications 1) are outside our control, 2) may be taken away from us at any moment by death, and 3) are not accessible to everyone.

-But there is another kind of gratification, the spiritual, the love for others, which 1) is always in our control, 2) is not taken from us by death, and we can die loving, and 3) not only is accessible to all, but the more people live for it, the more joy there will be."

- Tolstoy, *Last Diaries*

12 KEYS TO A CONTENTED LIFE ON ONE PAGE

- CULTIVATE A POSITIVE PERSPECTIVE
- TIME IS YOUR MOST VALUABLE RESOURCE – CHERISH IT
- SAVOUR LIFE'S JOYS
- CULTIVATE SOCIAL CONNECTIONS
- NURTURE AWARENESS MEDITATE
- PRACTICE KINDNESS & COMPASSION
- ACKNOWLEDGE SADNESS & DIFFICULTY
- DON'T BELIEVE YOUR THOUGHTS
- MAKE GOOD HABITS BREAK BAD HABITS
- THRIVE WHILE ALIVE... SLEEP
- BE GRATEFUL
- LIVE YOUR OWN STORY

THE BRAINY BITS ON ONE PAGE

MY PERCEPTION OF THE WORLD IS THE LENS THROUGH WHICH I LIVE

LOSSES LOOM LARGER THAN GAINS

BRAINS ARE PLASTIC

THE BRAIN SEEKS PATTERNS WHERE NONE EXIST

WE ARE NOT RATIONAL, LOGICAL BEINGS

NO MATTER HOW WE TRY OUR MIND WILL ALWAYS FIND PROBLEMS

OUR PERCEPTION IS NOT THE SAME AS REALITY

PREDICTION IS FLAWED AND MEMORY IS FAULTY

NOTES

INTRODUCTION
Alain de Botton, philosopher and author, founded The School of Life, an institute dedicated to understanding and improving our emotional intelligence. The School of Life is a collective of psychologists, philosophers and writers devoted to helping people lead calmer and more resilient lives. Have a look at their YouTube Channel
https://www.youtube.com/channel/UC7IcJI8PUf5Z3zKxnZvTBog

Chapter 1. IMPORTANCE OF A POSITIVE PERSPECTIVE
Measurement of Happiness: the most common way that researchers assess happiness is through self-reports. The rankings of national happiness are based on a Cantril ladder survey. Nationally representative samples of respondents are asked to think of a ladder, with the best possible life for them being a 10, and the worst possible life being a 0. They are then asked to rate their own current lives on that 0 to 10 scale. As happiness is generally measured subjectively at a single point in time, it is questionable how reliable they really are. We could have simply gotten up on the wrong side of the bed. Thus, having a generally more positive rather than negative outlook may be a better way of thinking of whether someone is a happy person or not.

Why is Positivity Important?
Positivity advantage - Multiple fringe benefits
    Health – stronger immune system - Taylor, S.E. & Armor, D.A. (1996). Positive illusion and coping with adversity. *Journal of Personality, 64:* 873-898. DOI: 10.1111/j.1467-6494.1996.tb00947.x
    Lower levels of stress-related hormones - Steptoe, A., Dockray, S. & Wardle, J. (2009). Positive Affect and Psychobiological Processes Relevant to Health, *Journal of Personality, 77(6):* 1747-76. DOI: 10.1111/j.1467-6494.2009.00599.x
    Higher levels of growth-related hormones - Berk, L.S., Tan, S.A., et al. (1989). Neuroendocrine and stress hormone changes during mirthful laughter. *American Journal of Medical Science, 298(6):* 390-6. DOI: 10.1097/00000441-198912000-00006
    Human gene expression – strong antibody & antiviral genes - Fredrickson BL, Grewen KM, Coffey KA, Algoe SB, Firestine AM, Arevalo JM, Ma J, Cole SW. (2013). A functional genomic perspective on human well-being. *Proceedings of the National Academy of Science U S A.* Aug 13;110(33):13684-9. DOI: 10.1073/pnas.1305419110
    Confidence levels - Brinol, P., Petty, R., & Barden, J. (2007). Happiness versus sadness as a determinant of thought confidence in persuasion: A self-validation analysis. *Journal of Personality and Social Psychology, 93 (5):* 711-727. DOI: 10.1037/0022-3514.93.5.711
    Better sleep - Ong, A. D., Exner-Cortens, D., Riffin, C., Steptoe, A., Zautra, A., & Almeida, D. (2013). Linking stable and dynami features of positive affect to sleep. *Annals of Behavioral Medicine, 46,* 52-61. DOI: 10.1007/s12160-013-9484-8
    Effective Coping & Conflict resolution - Waugh, C., Wager, T. et al. (2008). The neural correlates of trait resilience when anticipating and recovering from threat. *Social Cognitive and Affective Neuroscience, 3(4):* 322-332. DOI: 10.1093/scan/nsn024
    Relationships – sociability, likeability - Gable, S. L., Reis, H. T., Impett, E. A., & Asher, E. R. (2004). What do you do when things go right?: The intrapersonal and interpersonal benefits of sharing positive events. *Journal of Personality and Social Psychology, 87:* 228-245 DOI: 10.1037/0022-3514.87.2.228
    Work – higher income, less burnout, greater sales, superior productivity - Lyubomirsky, S., King, L. A., & Diener, E. (2005). The benefits of frequent positive affect: Does happiness lead to success? *Psychological Bulletin, 131:* 803-855. DOI: 10.1037/0033-2909.131.6.803
    Higher IQ - Rowe, G., Hirsh, J., & Anderson, A. (2007). Positive affect increases the breath of attentional selection. *Proceedings of the National Academy of Sciences of the United States of America,* 104: 383-88. DOI: 10.1073/pnas.0605198104
    Modulate cognition - Subramaniam K, Vinogradov S. (2013). Improving the neural mechanisms of cognition through the pursuit of happiness. *Frontiers of Human Neuroscience,* 20137:452. DOI: 10.3389/fnhum.2013.00452

Study on catching a cold and mood - Cohen S, Doyle WJ, Turner RB, Alper CM, Skoner DP.(2003). Emotional style and susceptibility to the common cold. *Psychosomatic Medicine,* 65(4):652-7. DOI: 10.1097/01.psy.0000077508.57784.da

Study on the nuns and longevity and Alzheimer's Disease –
Snowdon, David A. (2002). *Aging with Grace: What the Nun Study Teaches Us About Leading Longer, Healthier, and More Meaningful Lives.* New York, New York: Bantam Books.
  Moore, Bernardine A. (1995). Study of Nuns Turns up Clues to Brain Aging and Alzheimer's Disease. *Public Health Reports.* 110 (4): 508. DOI: *JSTOR 4597883*.

Link between positivity and health:
Positive psychology interventions appear to improve physical health. See
Park N, Peterson C, Szvarca D, Vander Molen RJ, Kim ES, Collon K. (2014). Positive Psychology and Physical Health: Research and Applications. *American Journal of Lifestyle Medicine*, 10(3):200-206.doi: 10.1177/1559827614550277. Note that more research is needed in this area.
  See also a review on how positive psychological interventions, which aim to cultivate psychological well-being, have the potential to improve health behavior adherence -
Feig EH, Madva EN, Millstein RA, Zambrano J, Amonoo HL, Longley RM ..Hoeppner B. (2022). Can positive psychological interventions improve health behaviors? A systematic review of the literature. *Preventative Medicine*, 163:107214. DOI: 10.1016/j.ypmed.2022.107214
  Positivity is linked to actual biological mechanisms. See Levy BR, Bavishi A. (2018). Survival Advantage Mechanism: Inflammation as a Mediator of Positive Self-Perceptions of Aging on Longevity. *Journal of the Gerontology, Psychological Sciences and Social Sciences,* 73(3):409-412. DOI: 10.1093/geronb/gbw035

What Determines Our Level of Happiness?
The source of the percentages of influence of genetics, circumstances and mindset to happiness is Lyubomirsky, S., Sheldon, K.M., & Schkade, D. (2005). Pursuing Happiness: The Architecture of Sustainable Change, *Review of General Psychology*, 9(2). https://doi.org/10.1037/1089-2680.9.2.111

Looking for happiness in all the wrong places
The research on lottery winners and accident victims - Brickman, P., Coates, D., & Janoff-Bulman, R. (1978). Lottery winners and accident victims: Is happiness relative? *Journal of Personality and Social Psychology, 36*(8), 917–927. https://doi.org/10.1037/0022-3514.36.8.917

Does having children make us happier? Some research indicates that parents are happier than nonparents, whereas others suggest the reverse. See Nelson, S.K., Kushlev, K. & Lyubomirsky, S. (2014). The pains and pleasures of parenting: when, why, and how is parenthood associated with more or less well-being? *Psychological Bulletin*, 140(3):846-895. DOI: 10.1037/a0035444
Myrskylä, M. & Margolis, R. (2014). Happiness: before and after the kids. *Demography*, 51(5):1843-66. DOI: 10.1007/s13524-014-0321-x

Some Things (Outside of Our Mental World) That Do Make Us Happier – Where We Live and How Spiritual We Are
  Tim Dean, Australian philosopher believes different places have different characters, and so pick one that suits your individual needs (if you could be said to be an individual, given cultural conditioning!) See his book *How We Became Human* (2021) Pan Macmillan Australia
  Many studies have uncovered a link between religion and life satisfaction, but all of the research faced a "chicken-and-egg problem". Does religion make people happy, or do happy people become religious? And if religion is the cause of life satisfaction, what is responsible — spirituality, social contacts, or other aspects? See Lim Chaeyoon, Putnam Robert D. (2010). Religion, social networks, and life satisfaction. *American Sociological Review*, 75:914–33. https://doi.org/10.1177/0003122410386686.
See also Deaton A, Stone AA. (2013). Two happiness puzzles. *American Economic Review*, 103(3):591-597. DOI: 10.1257/aer.103.3.591

Other things that might make us happier are our age, how much money we have, whether one is single or in a relationship? These issues are currently in debate
Are we happier at particular ages? Are younger folks happier than middle aged ones for example?
  Empirical literature has debated the existence of a so call U-shaped happiness-age curve. The idea is that happiness was highest among the younger and older cohorts with a nadir in midlife. However, on closer inspection, the research on this U curve is inconsistent, incomplete and is usually cross-sectional and not longitudinal. While some studies such as have found the whole U curve worldwide (e.g. Blanchflower DG. (2021). Is happiness U-shaped everywhere? Age and subjective well-being in 145 countries. *Journal of Population Economics*, 34(2):575-624. DOI: 10.1007/s00148-020-00797-

z), others have not (e.g. Steptoe A, Deaton A, Stone AA. (2015). Subjective wellbeing, health, and ageing. *Lancet.* 2;385(9968):640-648. DOI: 10.1016/S0140-6736(13)61489-0)

Does money make us happy? Are richer people happier than poorer people?
My mother had a saying *"You can only sleep in one bed and eat three meals a day"*. There is research to show that once a family has enough to live, they don't get much happier if they earn more. Kahneman D, Deaton A. (2010). High income improves evaluation of life but not emotional well-being. *Proceedings of the National Academy of Science U S A.*,107(38):16489-93. DOI: 10.1073/pnas.1011492107) .
However, there is also research which found that the more money people acquire, the happier they are. Killingsworth MA. (2021). Experienced well-being rises with income, even above $75,000 per year. *Proceedings of the National Acadademy of Science USA*, 118(4): e2016976118. DOI: 10.1073/pnas.2016976118

Does it make any difference to one's happiness whether one is single or in a relationship?
Some studies found those in a relationship are happier and healthier than singles e.g. Holt-Lunstad J, Birmingham W, Jones BQ. (2008). Is there something unique about marriage? The relative impact of marital status, relationship quality, and network social support on ambulatory blood pressure and mental health. *Annals of Behavioral Medicine,* 35(2):239-44. DOI: 10.1007/s12160-008-9018-y).
Others have found no influence on happiness. For example, researchers from Michigan State University conducted a study to measure the happiness of married, formerly married and single people at the end of their lives to find out just how much love and marriage played into overall wellbeing. The study examined the relationship histories of 7,532 people followed from ages 18 to 60 to determine who reported to be happiest at the end of their lives. Lifelong singles and those who had varied relationship histories didn't differ in how happy they were. The study's co-author, Mariah Purol said *"This suggests that those who have 'loved and lost' are just as happy towards the end of life than those who 'never loved at all.'"* If someone longs for a lifelong partner to start a family and build a happy life together, Chopik and Purol's research suggests that, if that individual isn't completely happy to begin with, it isn't likely that getting married will dramatically change anything. Purol MF, Keller VN, Oh J, Chopik WJ, Lucas RE. (2021). Loved and lost or never loved at all? Lifelong marital histories and their links with subjective well-being. *Journal of Positive Psychology,* 16(5):651-659. DOI: 10.1080/17439760.2020.1791946

The question of how positive we should actually be in order to be generally healthy and happy is a tricky one. It was believed that we only "thrived" if we were positive about 3 times more often than we were negative or miserable. This critical positivity ratio (also known as the "Losada ratio"), expounded in Barbara Frederick's book "Positivity" is now largely discredited.

The books cited in this section are
Castaneda, Carlos (1998) *The Teachings of Don Juan: A Yaqui Way of Knowledge.* Washington Square Press
Gilbert, Dan (2006) *Stumbling on Happiness.* Pub. Knopt
Gruman, Jamie & Deirdre Healey (2018) *Boost: The Science of Recharging Yourself in an Age of Unrelenting Demands.* Information Age Publishing
Lyubomirsky, Sonia (2007) *The How of Happiness: A practical approach to getting the life you want.* Great Britain: Sphere

CULTIVATE OPTIMISM

What Are You Paying Attention To? Depression among laywers. See Roth Port, D. (2018). Lawyers weigh in: Why is there a depression epidemic in the profession? *ABA (American Bar Association) Journal,* May 11, 2018
https://www.abajournal.com/voice/article/lawyers_weigh_in_why_is_there_a_depression_epidemic_in_the_profession

Martin Seligman (2004) *Authentic Happiness: Using the New Positive Psychology to Realize Your Potential for Lasting Fulfilment.* Simon & Schuster.

Benefits of Optimism -
One of the well-studied health-related positive psychology topics is optimism. Optimism is sometimes seen as Pollyanna-ism, a naively rosy view of the world coupled with a "don't worry, be happy" attitude. However, optimism the way researchers study it is a disposition to an expectation that the future will entail more positive events than negative ones. Optimists are neither in denial nor naive about challenges and difficulties in life. They simply attend to and acknowledge the positive.

Empirical research shows that optimism—usually assessed with self-report surveys—relates to better health and a lower chance of disease. A review of 15 studies found a 35% lower chance of getting heart disease and a 14% lower chance of early death in people who were optimists. See Rozanski A, Bavishi C, Kubzansky LD, Cohen R. (2019). Association of Optimism With Cardiovascular Events and All-Cause Mortality: A Systematic Review and Meta-analysis. *Journal of the American Medical Association, Network Open*, 2(9):e1912200. DOI: 10.1001/jamanetworkopen.2019.12200

Being optimistic is associated with biological risk factors such as lower blood sugar and cholesterol. See Hernandez R, Kershaw KN, Siddique J, Boehm JK, Kubzansky LD, Diez-Roux A, ..Lloyd-Jones DM. (2015). Optimism and Cardiovascular Health: Multi-Ethnic Study of Atherosclerosis (MESA). *Health Behavior Policy Review*, 2(1):62-73. DOI: 10.14485/HBPR.2.1.6

People who are optimistic also have better results following surgery, with fewer complications requiring hospital readmission. See Scheier MF, Matthews KA, Owens JF, Schulz R, Bridges MW, Magovern GJ, Carver CS. (1999). Optimism and rehospitalization after coronary artery bypass graft surgery. *Archives of Internal Medicine*, 159(8):829-35. DOI: 10.1001/archinte.159.8.829

Optimists have better coping skills when dealing with stress and setbacks. See Nes LS, Segerstrom SC. (2006). Dispositional optimism and coping: a meta-analytic review. *Personality and Social Psychology Review*, 10(3):235- 51. DOI: 10.1207/s15327957pspr1003_3

Cultivating optimism may boost your immunity and reduce chances of infection and cancer. See Kim ES, Hagan KA, Grodstein F, DeMeo DL, De Vivo I, Kubzansky LD.(2017). Optimism and Cause-Specific Mortality: A Prospective Cohort Study. *American Journal of Epidemiology*, 185(1):21-29. DOI: 10.1093/aje/kww182

Even after considering healthy behaviours, optimistic people had a 15% longer lifespan and 50% greater chance of living past 85 than people with a negative outlook. See Jacobs JM, Maaravi Y, Stessman J. Optimism and Longevity Beyond Age 85. (2021). *Journal of the Gerontology, Psychological Sciences and Social Sciences* (10):1806-1813. DOI: 10.1093/gerona/glab051

Among asymptomatic men with HIV, optimism slowed the onset of AIDS over an 18-month follow-up. See Reed GM, Kemeny ME, Taylor SE, Visscher BR. (1999). Negative HIV-specific expectancies and AIDS-related bereavement as predictors of symptom onset in asymptomatic HIV-positive gay men. *Health Psychology*, 18(4):354-63. DOI: 10.1037//0278-6133.18.4.354

A study of a large nationally representative sample of older adults (aged >50 years) in the United States showed that over a 2-year period, optimism predicted a lower likelihood of stroke, even after controlling for chronic illnesses, self-rated health, and relevant sociodemographic, biological, and psychological factors. See Kim ES, Park N, Peterson C. (2011). Dispositional optimism protects older adults from stroke: the Health and Retirement Study. *Stroke*, 42(10):2855-9. DOI: 10.1161/STROKEAHA.111.613448

Benefits of Positive Psychology Interventions -
Take note of What Went Well Today and Why? The landmark study conducted by Seligman and colleagues demonstrated the long-term benefits of positive psychology exercises. In the original study, two exercises administered over 1 week ("Three Good Things" and "Using your Signature Strengths in a New Way") were found to have long-lasting effects on depression and happiness. See Seligman, M.E.P., Steen, T.A., Park, N., Peterson, C. (2005). Positive psychology progress: Empirical validation of interventions. *American Psychologist*, 60, 410-421. DOI: 10.1037/0003-066X.60.5.410

These exercises have since been replicated (e.g. Mongrain M, Anselmo-Matthews T. (2012). Do positive psychology exercises work? A replication of Seligman et al. (2005). *Journal of Clinical Psychology*, 68(4):382-9. DOI: 10.1002/jclp.21839). Brief, positive psychology interventions may boost happiness through a common factor involving the activation of positive, self-relevant information. See also Carr, A., Finneran, L., Boyd, C., Shirey, C., Canning, C., Stafford, O., Lyons, J., Cullen, K., Prendergast, C., Corbett, C., Drumm, C., & Burke, T. (2023). The evidence-base for positive psychology interventions: A mega-analysis of meta-analyses. *Journal of Positive Psychology*.
https://doi.org/10.1080/17439760.2023.2168564

Our Brains Work like Lawyers, not Scientists
The School of Life – David Hume (https://www.theschooloflife.com/article/david-hume/)

Chapter 2. TAKE NOTE OF THE SMALL THINGS
People spend 'half their waking hours daydreaming'! The Harvard study can be found at Killingsworth MA, Gilbert DT. (2010). A wandering mind is an unhappy mind. *Science*, 330(6006):932. DOI: 10.1126/science.1192439

A wandering mind is an unhappy mind is supported by scientific findings, such as Hobbiss MH, Fairnie J, Jafari K, Lavie N. (2019). Attention, mindwandering, and mood. *Conscious Cognition*, 72:118. DOI: 10.1016/j.concog.2019.04.007).

However, other studies claim the opposite, unhappiness begets mind-wandering such as Poerio GL, Totterdell P, Miles E. (2013). Mind-wandering and negative mood: does one thing really lead to another? *Conscious Cognition*, 22(4):1412-21. DOI: 10.1016/j.concog.2013.09.012).

Others have even suggested that it's not a question of whether the mind wanders but where it wanders to. Smallwood J, O'Connor RC. (2011). Imprisoned by the past: unhappy moods lead to a retrospective bias to mind wandering. *Cognition and Emotion*, 25(8):1481-90. DOI: 10.1080/02699931.2010.545263)

NURTURE AWARENESS

Are You Paying Attention? The experiment carried out at Cornell University can be read at Simons, D.J. & Levin, D.T. (1998). Failure to detect changes to people during a real-world interaction. *Psychonomic Bulletin and Review*, 5(4), 644-649. DOI: 10.3758/BF03208840

The gorilla experiment - Simons, D.J., & Chabris, C.F. (1999). Gorillas in our midst: sustained inattentional blindness for dynamic events. *Perception*, 28, 1059-1074 DOI: 10.1068/p281059

THE POWER OF RITUAL

Works cited in this section are
Barker, Eric (2017) *Barking Up the Wrong Tree: The Surprising Science Behind Why Everything You Know About Success Is (Mostly) Wrong*. HarperCollins Publishers
Heath, Chip & Dan (2019) *The Power of Moments, Why Certain Experiences Have Extraordinary Impact*. Corgi Books

Research on the benefits of rituals
  Gino, F. & Norton, M.I. (2013). Why Rituals Work - There are real benefits to rituals, religious or otherwise. Scientific American, (published on May 14, 2013)
  Norton MI, Gino F. (2014). Rituals alleviate grieving for loved ones, lovers, and lotteries. *Journal of Experimental Psychology: General*, 143(1):266-72. DOI: 10.1037/a0031772
  Crespo C, Santos S, Canavarro MC, Kielpikowski M, Pryor J, Féres-Carneiro T. (2013). Family routines and rituals in the context of chronic conditions: a review. *International Journal of Psychology*, 48(5):729-46. DOI: 10.1080/00207594.2013.806811

Chapter 3. BE PRESENT, MEDITATE

Alan Watts (1987). *The Wisdom of Insecurity*. Ebury Publishing

Jon Kabat-Zinn is an American professor emeritus of medicine and the creator of the Stress Reduction Clinic and the Center for Mindfulness in Medicine, Health Care, and Society at the University of Massachusetts Medical School. He popularized mediation and mindfulness in the 1990s. The foundation of the curriculum of mindfulness-based stress reduction (MBSR), is outlined in *Full Catastrophe Living: Using the Wisdom of Your Body and Mind to Face Stress, Pain, and Illness* (2013, Bantam/Random House). This book articulated the transformative potential of cultivating mindfulness in one's own life in the face of stress, pain, and illness, and documented what was known at the time about its clinical effectiveness.

Read more about the proven benefits of regular meditation.
  Better Focus and Concentration
Researchers examined the brains of 16 people before and after participating in an eight-week meditation program with 17 controls who did not. Brain scans showed an increase in gray matter in the parts of the brain responsible for learning, memory, and emotional regulation compared to controls. Hölzel, B.K., Carmodyc, J., Vangela, M., Congletona, C., Yerramsettia, S.M., Garda, T. & Lazar, S.W. (2011). Mindfulness practice leads to increases in regional brain gray matter density. *Psychiatry Research: Neuroimaging*, 191, 36-43. https://isiarticles.com/bundles/Article/pre/pdf/32312.pdf
  Improve Self-Esteem and Reduce Anxiety
Goldin P, Ramel W, Gross J. (2009). Mindfulness Meditation Training and Self-Referential Processing in Social Anxiety Disorder: Behavioral and Neural Effects. *Journal of Cognitive Psychotherapy*, 23(3):242-257. DOI: 10.1891/0889-8391.23.3.242
  Reduce Stress

Khoury B, Lecomte T, Fortin G, Masse M, Therien P, Bouchard V, ..Hofmann SG.(2013). Mindfulness-based therapy: a comprehensive meta-analysis. *Clinical Psychology Review,* 33(6):763-71. DOI: 10.1016/j.cpr.2013.05.005

Manage Anxiety and Depression

Goyal M, Singh S, Sibinga EM, Gould NF, Rowland-Seymour A, Sharma R, ..Haythornthwaite JA. (2014). Meditation programs for psychological stress and well-being: a systematic review and meta-analysis. *JAMA Internal Medicine,* 174(3):357-68. DOI: 10.1001/jamainternmed.2013.13018

Helps Addiction

Prevent future relapses for people with a substance use disorder, as it produces a therapeutic effect that helps regulate how the brain experiences pleasure. Priddy SE, Howard MO, Hanley AW, Riquino MR, Friberg-Felsted K, Garland EL. (2018). Mindfulness meditation in the treatment of substance use disorders and preventing future relapse: neurocognitive mechanisms and clinical implications. *Substance Abuse and Rehabilitation,* 9:103-114. DOI: 10.2147/SAR.S145201 Brewer JA, Mallik S, Babuscio TA, et al. (2011). Mindfulness training for smoking cessation: results from a randomized controlled trial. *Drug and Alcohol Dependence,* 119(1–2):72–80. DOI: 10.1016/j.drugalcdep.2011.05.027

Helps Reduce Pain

Help to reduce pain in those who suffered from post-surgical, acute, or chronic pain. Garland EL, Brintz CE, Hanley AW, Roseen EJ, Atchley RM, Gaylord SA, ..Keefe FJ. (2020). Mind-Body Therapies for Opioid-Treated Pain: A Systematic Review and Meta-analysis. *JAMA Internal Medicine,* 180(1):91-105. DOI: 10.1001/jamainternmed.2019.4917

Chapter 4. ACKNOWLEDGE SADNESS AND DIFFICULTY

Works cited include

Didion, Joan (2005) *The Year of Magical Thinking.* Pub. Knopf

May, Katherine (2020) *Wintering: The Power of Rest and Retreat in Difficult Times.* Riverhead Books

Setiya, Kieran (2022) *Life is Hard, How Philosophy Can Help Us Find Our Way.* Penguin Random House.

Feeling bad about feeling bad can make you feel worse. Ford, B. Q., Lam, P., John, O. P., & Mauss, I. B. (2018). The psychological health benefits of accepting negative emotions and thoughts: Laboratory, diary, and longitudinal evidence. *Journal of Personality and Social Psychology, 115*(6), 1075–1092. https://doi.org/10.1037/pspp0000157

Notice feelings of pain - Maria Popova, *The Marginalian* - https://www.themarginalian.org/2021/03/06/wintering-katherine-may/

YOUR FLEXIBLE FRIEND - BRAINS ARE PLASTIC

"Neurons that fire together wire together" is commonly referred to as Hebb's Law. It attempts to connect the psychological and neurological underpinnings of learning. The basis is when our brains learn something new, neurons are activated and connected with other neurons, forming a neural network.

Books cited in this section include

Doidge, Norman (2007) *The Brain That Changes Itself: Stories of Personal Triumph from the Frontiers of Brain Science.* Pub. Viking.

Thornton, Elizabeth R. (2015) *The Objective Leader: How to Leverage the Power of Seeing Things As They Are.* St. Martin's Publishing Group

Weil, Andrew (1995) *Spontaneous Healing: How to Discover and Enhance Your Body's Natural Ability to Maintain and Heal Itself.* Knopf

Wimberger, Lisa (2012) *New Beliefs, New Brain: Free Yourself from Stress and Fear.* Divine Arts

Chapter 5. MAKE GOOD HABITS, BREAK BAD ONES

Duhigg, Charles (2012) *The Power of Habit: Why We Do What We -co- Do in Life and Business.* Random House

Research conducted at University College London by Phillippa Lally and colleagues - Lally, P., van Jaarsveld, C. H.M., Potts, H.W. & Wardle, J. (2001). How are habits formed: Modelling habit formation in the real world. *European Journal of Social Psychology,* 40(6), 998-1009. https://doi.org/10.1002/ejsp.674

CHANGING HABITS TO CHANGE YOUR LIFE

Books cited in this section are

Clear, James (2018) *Atomic Habits: An Easy & Proven Way to Build Good Habits & Break Bad Ones.* Penguin

Random House
Covey, Stephen (1989) *The 7 Habits of Highly Effective People*. Free Press.

Chapter 6. CULTIVATE GRATITUDE

Sample of studies on the benefits of gratitude:
Rash, J.A., Matsuba, M.K., & Prkachin, K.M. (2011). Gratitude and Well-Being: Who Benefits the Most from a Gratitude Intervention? *Applied Psychology: Health and Well-Being*, 3(3), 350-369. https://doi.org/10.1111/j.1758-0854.2011.01058.x
Toepfer, S. M., Cichy, K., & Peters, P. (2012). Letters of gratitude: Further evidence for author benefits. *Journal of Happiness Studies: An Interdisciplinary Forum on Subjective Well-Being*, 13(1), 187–201. https://doi.org/10.1007/s10902-011-9257-7
Emmons RA, McCullough ME. (2003). Counting blessings versus burdens: an experimental investigation of gratitude and subjective well-being in daily life. *Journal of Personality and Social Psychology*, 84(2):377-89. DOI: 10.1037//0022-3514.84.2.377
Seligman, M.E.P., Steen, T.A., Park, N., Peterson, C. (2005). Positive psychology progress: Empirical validation of interventions. *American Psychologist*, 60, 410-421. DOI: 10.1037/0003-066X.60.5.410

Managers who remember to say "thank you" to people who work for them may find that those employees feel motivated to work harder. Have a look at Grant AM, Gino F. (2010). A little thanks goes a long way: Explaining why gratitude expressions motivate prosocial behavior. *Journal of Personality and Social Psychology*, 98(6):946-55. DOI: 10.1037/a0017935

Research on gratitude to improve relationships: Lambert NM, Fincham FD. (2011). Expressing gratitude to a partner leads to more relationship maintenance behavior. *Emotion*, 11(1):52-60. DOI: 10.1037/a0021557

Camus, Albert (1994) *Le Premier Homme/ The First Man*. Editions Gallimard

OUR PERCEPTION IS NOT THE SAME AS REALITY

Naskar, Abhijit (2019) *Mission Reality*, Independently Published

Our Reality is What We Choose or are Conditioned to Perceive - This recent review summarizes a substantial placebo effect in 4925 patients with angina in seventy-eight randomized controlled trials (considered the gold standard design in scientific studies) across a variety of functional and life quality metrics - Gallone G, Baldetti L, Angelini F, ...De Ferrari GM. (2022).The Placebo Effect on Symptoms, Quality of Life, and Functional Outcomes in Patients With Angina Pectoris: A Meta-analysis of Randomized Placebo-Controlled Trials. *The Canadian Journal of Cardiology*, 38(1):113-122. DOI: 10.1016/j.cjca.2021.04.022

We See What We Want to See - Balcetis, E. & Dunning, D. (2006). See what you want to see: Motivational influences on visual perception. *Journal of Personality and Social Psychology*, 91(4): 612-25. DOI: 10.1037/0022-3514.91.4.612

I Know Why I Feel the Way I Do, Or Do I? - Dutton, D. & Aron, A. (1974). Some evidence for heightened sexual attraction under conditions of high anxiety, *Journal of Personality and Social Psychology*, 30(4): 510-17. DOI: 10.1037/h0037031

Psychologist Fritz Strack devised a simple experiment: Strack, F., Martin, L. L., & Stepper, S. (1988) Inhibiting and facilitating conditions of the human smile: A nonobtrusive test of the facial feedback hypothesis. *Journal of Personality and Social Psychology*, 54(5): 768-77. DOI: 10.1037//0022-3514.54.5.768
A 2019 review of 138 studies found that smiling influences people's emotions, but the effect was only small. Coles NA, Larsen JT, Lench HC. (2019). A meta-analysis of the facial feedback literature: Effects of facial feedback on emotional experience are small and variable. *Psychology Bulletin*, 145(6):610-651. DOI: 10.1037/bul0000194
A more recent study carried out in 19 countries found that the effect of smiling on our emotions is better if we mimic a photo of someone smiling or if we actually move the corners of our lips towards our ears rather than simply doing the pen-in-the-mouth task. Coles, N.A., March, D.S., Marmolejo-Ramos, F. et al. (2022). A multi-lab test of the facial feedback hypothesis by the Many Smiles Collaboration. *Nature Human Behaviour*, https://doi.org/10.1038/s41562-022-01458-9

Take home message, do "press ups" on the sides of your mouth or simply copy the smiling actor in the photo to lift your mood.

Chapter 7. LIVE EACH DAY LIKE A GROUNDHOG DAY

One of the most consistently observed phenomena in autobiographical memory research is the reminiscence bump: a tendency for middle-aged and elderly people to access more personal memories from approximately 10–30 years of age. See Munawar K, Kuhn SK, Haque S. (2018). Understanding the reminiscence bump: A systematic review. *PLoS One,* 13(12):e0208595. DOI: 10.1371/journal.pone.0208595

Books cited include
Burkeman, Oliver (2021) *Four Thousand Weeks.* Pub. Farrar, Straus and Giroux
Coelho, Pedro & M.J. Costa (2007). *The Witch of Portobello: a novel.* New York: Harper Collins Publishers.
Eagleman, David (2009) *Sum: Forty Tales from the Afterlife.* Publisher: Viking
Friedrich Nietzsche (1974) *The Gay Science/ The Joyful Wisdom/ The Joyous Science* (German: *Die fröhliche Wissenschaft*). Knopf Doubleday Publishing Group

FORGET BUSYNESS…ALLOW BOREDOM

Studies show boredom makes us more creative and productive. Neuroscientists James Danckert and Colleen Merrifield recruited some volunteers and put them into a neuroimaging scanner. They then induced those people into a mood of being bored. (They had them watch two men hanging laundry for eight minutes). When the participants were bored, a part of their brains called the "default mode network" fired on. It's a network of brain regions that activates when we're unfocused, when our mind is off and a key driver of creativity. It is a rest state that restores and rebuilds the resources needed to work better and more efficiently when we're focused on the outside world. Danckert, J., & Merrifield, C. (2018). Boredom, sustained attention and the default mode network." *Experimental Brain Research,* 236 (9), 2507-18. DOI: 10.1007/s00221-016-4617-5

More research on boredom and creativity: Mann, S. & Cadman, R. (2014) Does Being Bored Make Us More Creative? *Creative Research Journal,* 26(2), 165-173.
https://doi.org/10.1080/10400419.2014.901073

Chapter 8. CULTIVATE SOCIAL CONNECTIONS

The quality and quantity of individuals' social relationships has been linked to mental health (Cruwys T, Dingle GA, Haslam C, Haslam SA, Jetten J, Morton TA. (2013). Social group memberships protect against future depression, alleviate depression symptoms and prevent depression relapse. *Social Science & Medicine,* 98:179-86. DOI: 10.1016/j.socscimed.2013.09.013)

The 20-year longitudinal study in New Zealand can be read here: Saeri AK, Cruwys T, Barlow FK, Stronge S, Sibley CG. (2018). Social connectedness improves public mental health: Investigating bidirectional relationships in the New Zealand attitudes and values survey. *Australian and New Zealand Journal of Psychiatry,* 52(4):365-374. DOI: 10.1177/0004867417723990

The research from Stanford University School of Medicine showed that participating in support groups doesn't extend the lives of women with metastatic breast cancer, but did confirm that support groups improved quality of life for the participants, and showed a survival benefit for a subgroup of patients with an aggressive form of breast cancer. See Spiegel D, Butler LD, Giese-Davis J,… Kraemer HC. (2007). Effects of supportive-expressive group therapy on survival of patients with metastatic breast cancer: a randomized prospective trial. *Cancer,* 110(5):1130-8. DOI: 10.1002/cncr.22890

Studies have confirmed a connection between social connection and longevity. A robust body of scientific evidence has indicated that being embedded in high-quality close relationships and feeling socially connected to the people in one's life is associated with decreased risk for all-cause mortality as well as a range of disease morbidities. (Holt-Lunstad, J., Robles, T. F., & Sbarra, D. A. (2017). Advancing social connection as a public health priority in the United States. *American Psychologist, 72*(6), 517–530. https://doi.org/10.1037/amp0000103)

The review on social relationships and risk for mortality can be found here: Holt-Lunstad J, Smith TB, Layton JB. (2010). Social relationships and mortality risk: a meta-analytic review. *PLoS Medicine,* 7(7):e1000316. DOI: 10.1371/journal.pmed.1000316

We Are Not in This Alone - The research from Harvard Medical School on the "infectious" aspect of happiness - James H Fowler, N. & Christakis, A. (2008). Dynamic spread of happiness in a large social network: longitudinal analysis over 20 years in the Framingham Heart Study. *British Medical Journal*, 337:a2338 DOI: https://doi.org/10.1136/bmj.a2338

Social connections and obesity study - Christakis NA, Fowler JH. (2007). The spread of obesity in a large social network over 32 years. *New England Journal of Medicine*, 357(4):370-9.
DOI: 10.1056/NEJMsa066082

Social connections and smoking study - Christakis NA, Fowler JH. (2008). The collective dynamics of smoking in a large social network. *New England Journal of Medicine*, 358(21):2249-58. DOI: 10.1056/NEJMsa0706154

Are Social Media Connections Just as Good as Real-Life Relationships?
Negative associations between online social network use (in particular Facebook) and well-being. The University of Michigan study found that the more people used Facebook, the more their life satisfaction levels declined over time. "Interacting with other people "directly" did not predict these negative outcomes. They were also not moderated by the size of people's Facebook networks, their perceived supportiveness, motivation for using Facebook, gender, loneliness, self-esteem, or depression. On the surface, Facebook provides an invaluable resource for fulfilling the basic human need for social connection. Rather than enhancing well-being, however, these findings suggest that Facebook may undermine it." Kross, E., Verduyn, P., Demiralp, E., Park, J., Seungjae Lee, D., Linn, N., Shablack, H., Jonides, J. & Ybarra, O. (2013). Facebook Use Predicts Declines in Subjective Well-Being in Young Adults. *PLOS ONE*, https://doi.org/10.1371/journal.pone.0069841).
    Another study found that those who use Facebook believe that others are happier and have better lives than they do and the more time on Facebook each week, the more they believe this. Chou HT, Edge N. (2012)."They are happier and having better lives than I am": the impact of using Facebook on perceptions of others' lives. *Cyberpsychology, Behavior and Social Network*, 15(2):117-21. DOI: 10.1089/cyber.2011.0324
    Positive relationship between intensity of Facebook use and students' life satisfaction, social trust, civic engagement, and political participation. See study - Valenzuela, S., Park, N., & Kee, K. F. (2009). Is there social capital in a social network site?: Facebook use and college students' life satisfaction, trust, and participation. *Journal of Computer-mediated Communication*, 14(4), 875-901. https://doi.org/10.1111/j.1083-6101.2009.01474.x However, it should be noted that the authors stated *"While these findings should ease the concerns of those who fear that Facebook has mostly negative effects on young adults, the positive and significant associations between Facebook variables and social capital were small, suggesting that online social networks are not the most effective solution for youth disengagement from civic duty and democracy."*

LOSSES LOOM LARGER THAN GAINS...
MINE, MINE, MINE!
Watch the K Foundation burn a million quid on YouTube - https://www.youtube.com/watch?v=a3dcXzPFLOc

Research done at the National Research University Higher School of Economics, Moscow Gorin A, Krugliakova E, Nikulin V, Kuznetsova A, Moiseeva V, Klucharev V, Shestakova A. (2020). Cortical plasticity elicited by acoustically cued monetary losses: an ERP study. *Scientific Reports*, 10(1):21161. DOI: 10.1038/s41598-020-78211-7

Study done by psychologists at California Institute of Technology to test the extent the price tag of a bottle of wine influences how much we like it - Plassmann H, O'Doherty J, Shiv B, Rangel A. (2008) Marketing actions can modulate neural representations of experienced pleasantness. *Proceedings of the National Academy of Sciences U S A*. 105(3):1050-4. DOI: 10.1073/pnas.0706929105

An Italian study looked at the neural correlates of payment methods - Ceravolo MG, Fabri M, Fattobene L, Polonara G, Raggetti G. (2019) Cash, Card or Smartphone: The Neural Correlates of Payment Methods. Frontiers in Neuroscience, 5;13:1188. DOI: 10.3389/fnins.2019.01188

The famous dictum from Daniel Kahneman and Amos Tversky – see the original paper by Kahneman Daniel, and Tversky Amos (1979), Prospect Theory: An Analysis of Decisions Under Risk, *Econometrica*, 47(2), 263–91. http://www.jstor.org/stable/1914185

In 2007 psychologists at University of California Los Angeles found that brain regions that process value and reward may be silenced more when we evaluate a potential loss than they are activated when we assess a similar sized gain - see Tom SM, Fox CR, Trepel C, Poldrack RA. (2007). The neural basis of loss aversion in decision-making under risk. *Science*, 315(5811):515-8. DOI: 10.1126/science.1134239

Books cited are
Hammond, Claudia (2016) *Mind Over Money: The Psychology of Money and How to Use It Better*. Canongate Books
Schwartz, Barry (2014) *The Paradox of Choice: Why More Is Less*. Pub. Brilliance Audio

Chapter 9. KINDNESS AND COMPASSION

Practising kindness can help us feel calmer, less stressed and more positive. The British Columbian Study I mentioned can be found here - Alden L.E. & Trew, J.L. (2013). If it makes you happy: engaging in kind acts increases positive affect in socially anxious individuals. *Emotion*, 13(1):64-75. DOI: 10.1037/a0027761

Neuroimaging studies insinuate that Loving Kindness Meditation and Compassion Meditation may improve activation of brain areas that are involved in emotional processing and empathy. See Hofmann SG, Grossman P, Hinton DE. (2011). Loving-kindness and compassion meditation: potential for psychological interventions. *Clinical Psychological Review*, 31(7):1126-32. 10.1016/j.cpr.2011.07.003

Volunteering helps our health. See Kim, E.S., Whillans, A.V., Lee, M.T., Chen, Y. & VanderWeele, T.J. (2020) Volunteering and Subsequent Health and Well-Being in Older Adults: An Outcome-Wide Longitudinal Approach. *American Journal of Preventive Medicine*, 59(2), 176-186. https://doi.org/10.1016/j.amepre.2020.03.004

For more on kindness see –
Russell, Bernadette (2011) *The Little Book of Kindness: Everyday actions to change your life and the world around you*. Pub. Orion Pub. Co.
Newmark, Amy (2017) *Chicken Soup for the Soul: Random Acts of Kindness: 101 Stories of Compassion and Paying It Forward*. Pub. Amy New Mark

Abundance mentality can promote happiness and lead to more positive outcomes. Steffen L. (2009). Finding abundance in a world of scarcity. *Creative Nursing*, 15(2):66-9. DOI: 10.1891/1078-4535.15.2.66

In a large-scale longitudinal study on 18,000 people over a number of years, it was reported that envy is a powerful predictor of worse mental health. Mujcic, R., Oswald, A.J. (2018). Is envy harmful to a society's psychological health and wellbeing? A longitudinal study of 18,000 adults. *Social Science and Medicine*, 198:103-111.DOI: 10.1016/j.socscimed.2017.12.030

Envy results in a decline in wellbeing, Verduyn P, Lee DS, Park J, Shablack H, Orvell A, Bayer J, Ybarra O, Jonides J, Kross E. (2015). Passive Facebook usage undermines affective well-being: Experimental and longitudinal evidence. *Journal of Experimental Psychology General*, 144(2):480-8. https://doi.org/10.1037/xge0000057

Books cited were
Neff, Kristin (2011) *Self-Compassion Step by Step: The Proven Power of Being Kind to Yourself*. Pub. William Morrow
Polledri, Patricia (2012). *Envy in Everyday Life*. Clink Street Pub.

HOW MANY TIMES SHOULD WE FORGIVE?

Forgiveness is good for us. See Lawler KA., Younger JW, Piferi RL, Jobe RL, Edmondson KA, Jones WH. (2005). The unique effects of forgiveness on health: an exploration of pathways. *Journal of Behavioral Medicine*, 28:157-167

BRAINS SEEK PATTERNS WHERE NONE EXIST

Deacon, Terrance (1997) *The Symbolic Species: The co-evolution of language and the brain*. W.W. Norton & Company.
Shermer, Michael (2003) *How We Believe*. Times Books

Chapter 10. DON'T BELIEVE YOUR THOUGHTS
Fredrickson, Barbara (2013) *Love 2.0: How Our Supreme Emotion Affects Everything We Feel, Think, Do, and Become*. Penguin Publishing Group

For those who want to know some more about the Broaden and Build idea have a look at the following: Fredrickson B.L. (2004). The broaden-and-build theory of positive emotions. *Philosophical Transactions of the Royal Society of London Series B: Biological Sciences*, 359(1449):1367-78. DOI: 10.1098/rstb.2004.1512
Fredrickson B.L. (2001). The role of positive emotions in positive psychology. The broaden-and-build theory of positive emotions. *American Psychology*, 56(3):218- 26. https://doi.org/10.1037/0003-066X.56.3.218

If you want to feel good and get some understanding of how Cognitive Behavioural Therapy works, have a look at either of the following: David D. Burns, (1999) *Feeling Good: The New Mood Therapy*, Pub. William Morrow & Co. or Judith S. Beck, (2020) *Cognitive Behavior Therapy - Basics and Beyond*. Guilford Publications

The evidence-base of CBT is very strong. See for example - Hofmann SG, Asnaani A, Vonk IJ, Sawyer AT, Fang A. (2012). The Efficacy of Cognitive Behavioral Therapy: A Review of Meta-analyses. *Cognitive Therapy and Research*, 36(5):427-440. DOI: 10.1007/s10608-012-9476-1

Depressed individuals typically show poor memory for positive events and a bias retrieval towards negative events. Dillon DG, Pizzagalli DA. (2018). Mechanisms of Memory Disruption in Depression. *Trends in Neuroscience*, 41(3):137-149. DOI: 10.1016/j.tins.2017.12.006
However, depression also is associated with false memories of negative material – a double whammy for having the brain ski down the negativity slope! Joormann J, Teachman BA, Gotlib IH. (2009). Sadder and less accurate? False memory for negative material in depression. *Journal of Abnormal Psychology*, 118(2):412-7. DOI: 10.1037/a0015621

DON'T LET STRESS OVERWHELM YOU
Nestor, James (2020) *Breath: The New Science of a Lost Art*. Pub. Penguin Random House

Stress has a detrimental effect on us, both mentally and physically. See for example, Yaribeygi H, Panahi Y, Sahraei H, Johnston TP, Sahebkar A. (2017). The impact of stress on body function: A review. *EXCLI Journal: Experimental and Clinical Sciences*,16:1057-1072. DOI: 10.17179/excli2017-480

There are many studies on the benefits of breathing, Progressive Muscle Relaxation, and autogenics for stress. See for example –
Toussaint L, Nguyen QA, Roettger C, Dixon K, Offenbächer M, Kohls N, Hirsch J, Sirois F. (2021). Effectiveness of Progressive Muscle Relaxation, Deep Breathing, and Guided Imagery in Promoting Psychological and Physiological States of Relaxation. *Evidence Based Complementary & Alternative Medicine*, 5924040. DOI: 10.1155/2021/5924040
Ernst E, Kanji N. (2000). Autogenic training for stress and anxiety: a systematic review. *Complementary Therapies in Medicine*, 8(2):106-10. DOI: 10.1054/ctim.2000.0354

PREVENTATIVE MEASURES AGAINST STRESS
For more on expressive writing see James Pennebaker & John Evans (2014) *Expressive Writing: Words that Heal*, Pub. Idyll Arbor, Inc.

Rhythm and metaphor can tap into the less logical parts of our brain. See Mashal, N., Faust, M., Hendler, T., & Jung-Beeman, M.J. (2007). An fMRI investigation of the neural correlates underlying the processing of novel metaphoric expressions, *Brain and Language*, 100(2), 115-126. https://doi.org/10.1016/j.bandl.2005.10.005

The healing power of poetry can provide comfort and boost mood during periods of stress. For example, Delamerced, A., Panicker, C., Monteiro, K, & Chung, E.Y. (2021). see Effects of a Poetry Intervention on Emotional Wellbeing in Hospitalized Pediatric Patients. *Hospital Pediatrics*, 11, (3), 263-269.https://doi.org/10.1542/hpeds.2020-002535.
A systematic review published in 2020 found that poetry can help healthcare workers combat burnout and increase empathy for patients. Schoonover, K.L., Hall-Flavin, D., Whitford, K. et al. (2020). Impact of Poetry on Empathy and Professional Burnout of Health-Care Workers: A Systematic Review. *Journal of Palliative Care*, 35(2). https://doi.org/10.1177/0825859719865545)

Those interested in music therapy could have a look at - Li K, Weng L and Wang X (2021) The State of Music Therapy Studies in the Past 20 Years: A Bibliometric Analysis. *Frontiers in Psychology.* 12:697726. https://doi.org/10.3389/fpsyg.2021.697726

Benefits of Being in Nature -
Nature increases our creativity. For example, a University of Kansas study found that being in nature can boost your creativity by as much as 50 percent! Participants in the study spent four to six days immersed in nature and had to forgo all connections to technology. They explained that because of the tranquillity found in nature, our attention spans get a reset. In modern society, our brains never get a break from the overwhelming stimuli. See Atchley RA, Strayer DL, Atchley P. (2012). Creativity in the wild: improving creative reasoning through immersion in natural settings. *PLoS One,* 7(12):e51474 https://doi.org/10.1371/journal.pone.0051474
Nature can ease stress. Living closer to our natural environment can make us calmer. For example, a study found that adults in Scotland who lived closer to more greenery had lower levels of cortisol. See Roe JJ, Thompson CW, Aspinall PA, Brewer MJ, Duff EI, Miller D, Mitchell R, Clow A. (2013). Green space and stress: evidence from cortisol measures in deprived urban communities. *International Journal of Environmental Research and Public Health,* 10(9):4086-103.
DOI: 10.3390/ijerph10094086
Living in greener areas improves mental health. See for example, Alcock I, White MP, Wheeler BW, Fleming LE, Depledge MH. (2014). Longitudinal effects on mental health of moving to greener and less green urban areas. *Environmental Science & Technology,* 48(2):1247-55.
DOI: 10.1021/es403688w
Nature heals. For example, see Ulrich, R.S. (1984). View through a window may influence recovery from surgery. *Science,* 224(4647):420-1. DOI: 10.1126/science.6143402

Some research on the positive impact of laughter on both our physiology and psychology. Louie, D., Brook, K., Frates, E. (2016). The Laughter Prescription: A Tool for Lifestyle Medicine. *American Journal of Lifestyle Medicine,* 10(4):262-267. doi: 10.1177/1559827614550279
Dunbar RIM, Baron R, Frangou A, et al. (2012). Social laughter is correlated with an elevated pain threshold. Proceedings. Biological sciences, 279:1161-1167 DOI: 10.1098/rspb.2011.1373
Takahashi, K., Iwase, M., Yamashita, K., et al. (2001). The elevation of natural killer cell activity induced by laughter in a crossover-designed study. *International Journal of Molecular Medicine,* 8:645-650. DOI: 10.3892/ijmm.8.6.645
Nadler, R.T., Rabi, B., Minda, J.P. (2010). Better mood and better performance. Learning rule-described categories is enhanced by positive mood. *Psychological Science,* 21:1770-1776. DOI: 10.1177/0956797610387441

NO MATTER HOW WE TRY, OUR MIND WILL ALWAYS FIND PROBLEMS
Bell, Joanna Franklin (2012) *Take a Load Off, Mona Jamborski.* Createspace Independent Pub

Harvard psychologist David Levari showed people hundreds of images of faces - Levari DE, Gilbert DT, Wilson TD, Sievers B, Amodio DM, Wheatley T. (2018). Prevalence-induced concept change in human judgment. *Science,* 360(6396):1465-1467. DOI: 10.1126/science.aap8731

Chapter 11. IF YOU WANT TO THRIVE WHILE ALIVE.... SLEEP
Satchin Panda (2018) *Circadian Code: Lose Weight, Supercharge Your Energy, and Transform Your Health from Morning to Midnight.* Ebury Publishing

Lots of research supports the importance of respecting our circadian rhythm for our health. See for example, Scott AJ. (2000). Shift work and health. *Primary Care,* 27(4):1057-79. DOI: 10.1016/s0095-4543(05)70189-5
Walker WH 2nd, Walton JC, DeVries AC, Nelson RJ. (2020). Circadian rhythm disruption and mental health. *Translational Psychiatry,* 10(1):28. DOI: 10.1038/s41398-020-0694-0

Research has found that sleep disruption predicts cognitive decline. Accumulation in the brain of a protein, Amyloid-β (Aβ) is a hallmark of Alzheimer's disease. During deep sleep, the brain appears to wash away waste products, such as β-Amyloid, that increase the risk for Alzheimer's disease. See for example, Winer, J.R., Mander, B.A., Kumar, S.,... & Walker, M.P. (2020). Sleep Disturbance Forecasts β-Amyloid Accumulation across Subsequent Years. *Current Biology,* 30(21), 4291-98. DOI: https://doi.org/10.1016/j.cub.2020.08.017.

See also Simon Makin's article in *Scientific American* (Dec 16, 2016). Why Sleep Disorders May Precede Parkinson's and Alzheimer's.

Studies claim that sleep duration has declined over the last 50 years e.g.
Matricciani L., Olds, T. & Petkov, J. (2012). In search of lost sleep: secular trends in the sleep time of school-aged children and adolescents. *Sleep Medicine Review*, 16(3):203-11. DOI: 10.1016/j.smrv.2011.03.005.
Ford E.S., Cunningham T.J. & Croft, J.B. (2015). Trends in Self-Reported Sleep Duration among US Adults from 1985 to 2012. *Sleep*, 38(5):829-32. DOI: 10.5665/sleep.4684).
However, others have found no such drastic trends (Youngstedt SD, Goff EE, Reynolds AM, Kripke DF, Irwin MR, Bootzin RR, Khan N, Jean-Louis G. (2016). Has adult sleep duration declined over the last 50+ years? *Sleep Medicine Review*, 69-85. DOI: 10.1016/j.smrv.2015.08.004)

Yoga for Insomnia. See Khalsa, S.B. (2004). Treatment of chronic insomnia with yoga: a preliminary study with sleep-wake diaries. *Applied Psychophysiology and Biofeedback*. 29(4):269-78. DOI: 10.1007/s10484-004-0387-0
Wang, X., Li, P., Pan, C., Dai, L., Wu, Y., Deng, Y. (2019. The Effect of Mind-Body Therapies on Insomnia: A Systematic Review and Meta-Analysis. *Evidence Based Complementary & Alternative Medicine*, 9359807. DOI: 10.1155/2019/9359807

Research suggests that caffeine taken up to 6 hours before bedtime has important disruptive effects on sleep (Drake, C., Roehrs, T., Shambroom, J. & Roth, T. (2013). Caffeine effects on sleep taken 0, 3, or 6 hours before going to bed. *Journal of Clinical Sleep Medicine*, 9(11):1195-1200. https://doi.org/10.5664/jcsm.3170)

A 2018 study compared the sleep quality among people who consumed different amounts of alcohol. Pietilä, J., Helander, E., Korhonen, I., Myllymäki, T., Kujala, U.M. & Lindholm, H. (2018). Acute Effect of Alcohol Intake on Cardiovascular Autonomic Regulation During the First Hours of Sleep in a Large Real-World Sample of Finnish Employees: Observational Study. *JMIR Mental Health*, 1616;5(1):e23 DOI: 10.2196/mental.9519
   The findings are as follows: Low amounts of alcohol (fewer than two servings per day for men or one serving per day for women) decreased sleep quality by 9.3%. Moderate amounts of alcohol (two servings per day for men or one serving per day for women) decreased sleep quality by 24%. High amounts of alcohol (more than two servings per day for men or one serving per day for women) decreased sleep quality by 39.2%.
   To reduce the risk of sleep disruptions, you should stop drinking alcohol at least four hours before bedtime. (Stein M.D. & Friedmann, P.D. (2005). Disturbed sleep and its relationship to alcohol use. *Substance Abuse*, 26(1):1-13. DOI: 10.1300/j465v26n01_01)

A broad body of evidence indicates that being exposed to light at night may be harmful not only to sleep, but in a variety of ways and could predispose people to chronic diseases. (Cho Y, Ryu SH, Lee BR, Kim KH, Lee E, Choi J. (2015). Effects of artificial light at night on human health: A literature review of observational and experimental studies applied to exposure assessment. *Chronobiology International*, 32(9):1294-310. DOI: 10.3109/07420528.2015.1073158).

Naps help our cognitive performance. See Mednick S, Nakayama K, Stickgold R. (2003). Sleep-dependent learning: a nap is as good as a night. *Nature Neuroscience*, 6(7):697-8. DOI: 10.1038/nn1078. See Dr Sara Mednick's TED talk "Give it up for the down state – sleep" on sleep research and importance of healthy sleep hygiene. https://youtu.be/MklZJprP5F0

There are so many research papers on how many hours we should sleep. Here are a few for those who are interested.
   Watson NF, Badr MS, Belenky G, Bliwise DL, Buxton OM, Buysse D, ...Tasali E. (2015). Recommended amount of sleep for a healthy adult: a joint consensus statement of the American Academy of Sleep Medicine and Sleep Research Society. *SLEEP*, 38(6):843–844.
   Chaput JP, Dutil C, Sampasa-Kanyinga H. (2018). Sleeping hours: what is the ideal number and how does age impact this? *Nature and Science of Sleep*.10:421-430.

THE FABRICATED PAST AND THE IMAGINARY FUTURE
Kerouac, Jack (1995) *The Portable Jack Kerouac*. Penguin Classics

The research on eyewitness memory can be found here - Loftus, E. F., & Palmer, J. C. (1974). Reconstruction of automobile destruction: An example of the interaction between language and memory. *Journal of Verbal Learning & Verbal Behavior*, 13(5), 585–589. https://doi.org/10.1016/S0022-5371(74)80011-3

For more on false memory see *The Science of False Memory* by Charles Brainerd and Valerie Reyna (2005, Oxford University Press). This book encompasses and weaves together the common threads of the four major topics that comprise the core of false memory research: theories of false memory, adult experimental psychology of false memory, false memory in legal contexts, and false memory in psychotherapy. It provides a comprehensive picture of our current understanding of human false memory.

More information on the Innocence Project see Eyewitness Identification Reform https://innocenceproject.org/eyewitness-identification-reform/

Flashback memory study on Sept 11: Hirst, W., Phelps, E.A., Meksin, R., Vaidya, C.J., Johnson, M.K., Mitchell, K.J., .. Olsson, A. (2015). A ten-year follow-up of a study of memory for the attack of September 11, 2001: Flashbulb memories and memories for flashbulb events. *Journal of Experimental Psychology General*, 144(3):604-23.

We spend much of our day thinking about the future. See D'Argembeau, A., Renaud, O., & Van der Linden, M. (2011). Frequency, characteristics and functions of future-oriented thoughts in daily life. *Applied Cognitive Psychology*, 25(1), 96-103. https://doi.org/10.1002/acp.1647

Research on Tattoos - see Liszewski, W., Kream, E., Helland, S., Cavigli, A., Lavin, B.C. & Murina, A. (2015). The Demographics and Rates of Tattoo Complications, Regret, and Unsafe Tattooing Practices: A Cross-Sectional Study. *Dermatological Surgery*, 41(11):1283-9. DOI: 10.1097/DSS.0000000000000500

Chapter 12. LIVE YOUR OWN STORY

This study found that inducing a positive mood among physicians improved their creative problem solving and influenced their practice satisfaction - Estrada C. A., Young M., Isen A. M. (1994). Positive affect influences creative problems solving and reported source of practice satisfaction in physicians. *Motivation and Emotion*, 18, 285–299 https://doi.org/10.1007/BF02856470).

Women are more likely to have an affair when ovulating than at any other time of the month. See for example - Gangestad, S.W., Thornhill, R. & Garver-Apgar, C.E. (2005). Women's sexual interests across the ovulatory cycle depend on primary partner developmental instability. *Proceedings of Biological Science.*;272(1576):2023-7. DOI: 10.1098/rspb.2005.3112

For anyone interested in the Dunning-Kruger effect, a cognitive bias whereby people overestimate their own knowledge or competence in a domain relative to objective criteria or to the performance of their peers or of people in general see Alicke Mark D., Govorun Olesya. The better-than-average effect. In: Alicke Mark D., Dunning David, Krueger Joachim I., editors. *The Self in Social Judgment*. Psychology Press; Hove: 2005. pp. 85–106.

In America most people overestimate their IQ. See Heck P.R., Simons D.J. & Chabris, C.F. (2018). 65% of Americans believe they are above average in intelligence: Results of two nationally representative surveys. *PLoS One*. 3;13(7) DOI: 10.1371/journal.pone.0200103
    This self-inflation on IQ tends to be more of a Western than a universal phenomenon. In research comparing North American and East Asian self-assessments, Heine of the University of British Columbia finds that East Asians tend to underestimate their abilities, with an aim toward improving the self and getting along with others. Heine SJ, Hamamura T. (2007). In search of East Asian self-enhancement. *Personality and Social Psychology Review*, 11(2):204. DOI: 10.1177/1088868306294587

Affirmations - Good article by Donald Altman in *Psychology Today* (Sept, 2022) on affirmations (*Plant Mind Seeds to Reprogram Negative Habits -Your subconscious can help you overcome harmful lifestyle habits*. https://www.psychologytoday.com/us/blog/practical-mindfulness/202209/plant-mind-seeds-reprogram-negative-habits
    A study showed that self-affirmations activated brain networks related to one's sense of identity, as well as predicting changes in sedentary behaviour (Cascio, C.N., Brook O'Donnell, M., Tinney, F.J., Lieberman, M.D., Taylor, S.E., ...& Falk, E.B. (2016). Self-affirmation activates brain

systems associated with self-related processing and reward and is reinforced by future orientation. *Social Cognitive and Affective Neuroscience*, 621–629 DOI: 10.1093/scan/nsv136)

Works cited in this section are
Bruner, Jerome (1987). Life as Narrative, *Social Research*, 54, 11-32, 15
Hood, Bruce (2012) *The Self Illusion: How the Social Brain Creates Identity*. Oxford University Press
McAdams, Dan & Erika Manczak (2015) *APA Handbook of Personality and Social Psychology*. APA
Sacks, Oliver (1985) *The Man Who Mistook His Wife for a Hat*. Gerald Duckworth Pub.
Wilson, Timothy (2004) *Strangers to Ourselves Discovering the Adaptive Unconscious*. Harvard University Press.

LIFE IS A SERIES OF "NOWS" THAT ENDS IN DEATH

The study by the researchers at the University of Kentucky and Florida State University was DeWall, C.N. & Baumeister, R.F. (2007). From terror to joy: automatic tuning to positive affective information following mortality salience. *Psychological Science*, 18(11):984-90. DOI: 10.1111/j.1467-9280.2007.02013.x

Books cited include
Easter, Michael (2021) *The Comfort Crisis: Embrace Discomfort to Reclaim Your Wild, Happy, Healthy Self*. Rodale Books
Castaneda, Carlos (1974) *Journey to Ixtlan: The Lessons of Don Juan*. Pocket Books
Watts, Alan (1987). *The Wisdom of Insecurity*. Ebury Publishing

REWRITING OUR STORIES OF OTHERS

Deaf with a capital D indicates a cultural identity for people with hearing loss who share a common culture and sense of identity and who usually have a shared sign language. The word deaf is used to describe or identify anyone who has a severe hearing problem. Sometimes it is used to refer to people who are severely hard of hearing too.

Books cited include
Dreger, Alice (2004) *One of Us: Conjoined Twins and the Future of Normal*. Harvard University Press
Sacks, Oliver (1995) *An Anthropologist on Mars*. Pub. Alfred A. Knopf

WE ARE NOT AS UNIQUE OR AS CONSISTENT AS WE THINK

The Barnum effect, or Forer effect, is a common psychological phenomenon whereby people give high accuracy ratings to descriptions of their personality that are supposedly tailored individually to them, yet which are in fact vague and general enough to apply to a wide range of people. Such an effect may partially explain why we accept what we are told by astrology and fortune telling readings, and indeed some personality tests.

"YOU ARE GOOD ENOUGH"

I read a range of "self-help" /pop psychology books such as -
Covey, Stephen (1989) *The 7 Habits of Highly Effective People*. Free Press.
Carnegie, Dale (1937) *How to win friends and influence people*. Simon & Schuster, Penguin Publishing
Frankl, Victor (1962) *Man's Search for Meaning*. Abe Books.
Brown, Brené (2015) *Daring Greatly: How the Courage to Be Vulnerable Transforms the Way We Live, Love, Parent, and Lead*. Penguin Publishing Group
Robbins, Tony (1991) *Awaken the Giant Within*. Simon & Schuster.
Tolle, Eckhart (1997) *The Power of Now*. Namaste Publishing
Tolle, Eckhart (2005) *A New Earth: Awakening to Your Life's Purpose*. Dutton
Seligman, Martin (2004) *Authentic Happiness: Using the New Positive Psychology to Realize Your Potential for Lasting Fulfilment*. Simon & Schuster.

AFTERWORD

Harari, Yuval Noah (2011) *Sapiens: A Brief History of Humankind*. Random House Harper
Tolstoy, Leo (author); Leon Stilman (editor) (1960) *Last Diaries*. Capricorn Books.

About the Author

Mary Flaherty PhD is a psychologist, life coach, researcher, yoga teacher, science communicator and world wanderer.

Her passion for teaching and her academic career have taken her to universities in Japan, Singapore, Australia, the United States, South America and Europe. Her research articles, published in peer-reviewed journals are on topics as diverse as the effect of yoga on low back sensitivity, to how sign language influences cognition. She is the author of "Does Yoga Work? Answers from Science". She is an unashamed nerd, and likes nothing better than curling up with a pile of research papers to read.

Instagram: @marydoesyoga

Printed in Poland
by Amazon Fulfillment
Poland Sp. z o.o., Wrocław